GOD
OF THE
VALLEYS

GOD
OF THE
VALLEYS

*Heaven's High Purpose
for Your Lowest Times*

MARK RUTLAND

SERVANT PUBLICATIONS
ANN ARBOR, MICHIGAN

Vine Books is an imprint of Servant Publications especially designed to serve evangelical Christians.

Scripture passages quoted in this book are taken from the King James Version of the Bible.

To protect the privacy of some of the individuals whose stories are told in this book, names and characterizations have been fictionalized, although they are based on real events.

Published by Servant Publications
P.O. Box 8617
Ann Arbor, Michigan 48107

Cover design: Left Coast Design, Portland, Oregon
Cover illustration: Cecil Rice, Acworth, Georgia

00 01 02 03 10 9 8 7 6 5 4 3 2 1

Printed in the United States of America
ISBN 1-56955-175-8

LIBRARY OF CONGRESS CATALOGING-IN-PUBLICATION DATA

Rutland, Mark.
    God of the valleys / by Mark Rutland.
        p. cm.
    ISBN 1-56955-175-8 (alk. paper)
    1. Spiritual life—Christianity. 2. Christian life. 3. Kings and rulers—
Biblical teaching. I. Title.

BV4501.2 .R857 2000
248.8'6—dc21   00-042859

For my children,
Travis, Rosemary, and Emily,
in whom I delight.

CONTENTS

THE RIO MANTARO
VALLEY, PERU

Sentries standing silent guard duty along pebbled banks, the massive eucalyptus trees fearlessly hurl their purple shadows out across the violent, rocky stream. The Rio Mantaro first slithers down a high, lush mountain valley from Huancayo to the eastern slope of the Andes, then plunges recklessly down into the vast jungled lap of South America. Fed by frigid mountain springs and melting snow, the trout-filled river gnaws with relentless futility at the granite walls of its confinement.

Old women, sprung from and hardly unlike the ancient Incas slain by treacherous conquistadors, lead lines of dour llamas along tracks etched in the unforgiving Andean hide. Descendants herd descendants along paths as old as Egypt. Wide flat brims on the women's embroidered hats shield their brown faces from a reluctant, misty-eyed sun that only occasionally winks out by whimsy, barely warming the high valley's chilly mountain hamlets.

Cool on its warmest day, eleven thousand feet in the sky at its lowest point, the mountain valley of the Mantaro River enfolds past and present in its green embrace. This is not some sweet romantic little hug, but a ferocious passion that mocks at modern distinctions between "then" and "now." The river, timeless and unstoppable, burbles along, new and rowdy, across the toes of giggling fisher boys and the souls of Inca chieftains.

Every life, all of history, is a valley with a river down its length.

One

THE GOD OF THE VALLEYS

My wife somehow coaxed me into one of those modern American halls of torture called a shopping mall, then beckoned me by her multiple charms to stand benignly amidst the racks along with all the other cowed husbands loitering there in such obvious discomfort. She and the other wives tried on clothes in the inner sanctum; we males avoided one another's eyes yet recognized each other as the company of the domesticated. We held in our hands not shotguns or golf clubs but the bulging plastic bag repositories of modern consumer culture. Adventurers who should have been scouting with Kit Carson or defending the Alamo with Crockett and Bowie, we were instead pack animals wearing our burdens and our domesticity like thorny crowns.

Searching for some distraction from my bondage, I became desperate enough to read the labels on clothing hung on the racks. This, along with the backs of cereal boxes, is the sub-basement of literature. How surprising that there, amidst all the warnings to dry-clean only, I should find one of the great truths of life.

One tag—not content to merely catalogue the percentages of the various materials used, such as 30-percent wool, 50-percent rayon, 20-percent God-knows-what—had risen to the challenge by making a philosophical statement of such merit that I quote it here.

This fabric woven of natural fibers.
The irregularities only enhance the beauty of your garment.

We Westerners lust for a life of seamless luxury, mountaintop-to-mountaintop splendor, so perfect and painless that we never have to endure or conquer or overcome anything. In so doing, we have made ourselves into a tribe of weaklings. The smooth plasticity of suburban life is culture in a beanbag chair: low, soft, and virtually impossible to get out of.

As soon as our parents or grandparents cross that invisible line from senior citizenship to the far uglier state of elderly, we shut them away, not a part of the irregularities, but an unfortunate and distant fact to be visited, then forgotten. Grandpa no longer lives in the house, totters down to breakfast, makes the same tired jokes at every meal, and sits whittling on the front porch. He is in a nursing home in Fort Lauderdale counting the minutes to heaven or lunch, whichever comes first. He does not live with us and he certainly does not die with us, and most likely we will not attend his funeral. That would be too, too painful.

We will not walk through valleys. We abort inconvenient babies and unfulfilling marriages with a casualness that sets a premium on comfort and dismisses life and commitment as painful relics, the Shaker chairs of a bankrupt value system, quaint antiques on display but never actually to be sat in. The tragedy? Valleys give life the rich lushness of definition. From mountaintops we view life; in valleys we live it. Valleys are where farms get plowed, babies get born, and the dead are buried.

Valleys can be dry gulches, terrifying deserts, or wide, rich plains that stretch across the floor of the earth for miles. Peaceful or frightening, jungled swamps or grassy plains, valleys are the cradle of life, the irregularities that enhance the beauty of your garment.

God's Testimony in 1 Kings 20

When Ben-hadad, the King of Syria, marched into Israel, he expected nothing more than token resistance. Israel's capital of Samaria, though a prosperous and formidable walled city, could boast an army of less than ten thousand defenders. Ben-hadad rode at the head of thirty-two armies, each commanded by a subking, a mighty alliance of tens of thousands of infantry plus cavalry and chariots.

For his part, Israel's King Ahab, no sterling hero to be sure, was willing to pay a hefty tribute to avoid utter devastation at the hands of so mighty a host. Weakened by his own wickedness and his unlawful marriage to Jezebel, Ahab lacked both the resolve to fight and the faith to believe God for a miracle. He was quite ready to pay for survival.

What he was not ready for was the demand of Ben-hadad. The Syrian messengers at the gate were terrifying. Ben-hadad's ferocious, swarthy emissaries of horror with scimitars at their sides sat effortlessly on their prancing Arabian steeds. It seemed to the Israeli defenders on the wall that even the horses were eager for battle and blood.

"The gates must be opened. Every man, from King to peasant, must stand aside while we loot the city. You must watch while we enter every house in the city and carry away everything we desire of your gold, your possessions, and your women. Everything! That is the tribute of Ben-hadad. Accept it or be destroyed."

Shock settled on the city and King Ahab like a cloud. Never had such a tribute been demanded. Grim-faced elders gathered in royal conference to offer their counsel but each knew that there could be only one answer. The Syrians had made an impossible demand. If the invaders were going to loot the city anyway, Israel may as well fight. Surely once Ben-hadad's army was in the city they would not stop with looting and rape. Resistance seemed futile, but voluntary genocide was the alternative.

"Your Majesty," one elder said. "Don't listen to this absurd demand."

"That's right, sire," offered another. "To submit to this means the death of us all and the destruction of Israel."

The council was unanimous. Any unreasonable tribute would have been paid, but this was not tribute; this was certain death. If they were going to die anyway, they may as well die fighting.

The Syrian messengers were surprised and gratified to see King Ahab himself on the wall. This must mean that he was willing to capitulate. He could have sent an emissary with a rejection.

"Tell my lord, King Ben-hadad, that we were willing to pay, even a great deal. He had but to make any reasonable demand. But this we cannot do. Samaria is closed up. Let him besiege us if he will, but we will not open the gates to such a demand."

Without a word the Syrian delegation spun their horses and

charged toward their own lines. King Ahab and the elders on the wall silently watched them leave, each man struggling with his own fears and misgivings. Had they done the right thing? No matter now. What lay ahead was the nightmare of an extended siege, the slow war of constant attack, disease, and starvation. Their walls could probably not be breached, but how long could they hold out inside? They peered out at the tents of the Syrians, impossible to count, and worried that it was not long.

Then began the psychological warfare, the taunting and intimidation by which each king hoped to weaken the resolve of the other. It was a ritual of terror, the minuet of death danced at a distance by enemies, not lovers. Ben-hadad sent a message to Ahab, saying, "Look at our armies. We are an alliance of thirty-two kings with all their strength. Look at us. We have spies and we know what you have. Compared to us, your little army of seven thousand is but two handfuls of dust."

Ahab's response was more creative perhaps, but no more subtle. "Strap on your armor. But remember, when a soldier is dead on the battlefield, someone else takes it off."

That served only to infuriate the Syrian warlord who ordered that siege lines be set. So it began. The long, mostly boring war of attrition that was nearly as hard on the attackers as on the city was now to start in earnest. First, a prewar orgy of alcohol would boost the spirits of his leaders. They gathered in the evening of the first day of the siege and, by noon the next day, King Ben-hadad and his coterie of thirty-two kings were staggering, blind drunk in the royal pavilion.

At noon sentries reported an Israeli delegation of exactly thirty-two had left the city and was riding straight for the Syrian lines. Ben-hadad, his speech slurred and his judgment impaired, ordered that they be admitted to his tent. The bloodbath in the tent was immediate and dreadful. The screams and curses of drunken men unable to defend themselves plunged the Syrian camp into a panic, just as the entire seven-thousand-man army of Israel erupted from the close cover of the wadis and poured down on the dozing, hung-over Syrians like hot lava.

Of all the kings that rode out with Ben-hadad, only he himself escaped. The slaughter of the Syrians was monstrous. Corpses strewn like excess baggage lay behind the mad retreat for miles, while hamstrung horses screamed and the smoke of burning chariots polluted the midday sky.

The Israeli victory was absolute, but temporary. Ben-hadad was gone but still alive and Israel knew that he would surely come again. The next time he would not be so easily tricked.

In Damascus, the furious and vengeful king summoned his war council and demanded an explanation for the embarrassing and crushing defeat. If anyone dared to reason that it had anything to do with the king and his entire military leadership getting so falling-down drunk that a substantial enemy commando was invited to a party, he kept that thought to himself. Instead, one diplomatic adviser offered a more spiritual reason.

"Your Majesty," the vizier explained. "Samaria is on a mountaintop. That was the cause of our defeat. The god of Israel is a god of mountains, not of valleys. If we can but lure them out of their city, down into the valleys and plains below, their god cannot protect them there."

This was good stuff, music to Ben-hadad's ears. It was logical and strategic, with a spiritual air about it that he really liked. Certainly this was right. A god of mountains could not also be the god of valleys. Ben-hadad began to feel better about the whole thing. An expensive lesson had been learned, but now he could not wait for spring. This campaign would be successfully fought in a valley, where their god would be impotent to help.

"Furthermore, Your Majesty," the vizier continued. "Let the kings be replaced with real military men."

Ah, that was good, too. Ben-hadad saw at that moment that much of the blame for the defeat could be laid on incompetent subordinates. This adviser was good, very good, and Ben-hadad would remember to reward him.

Their reasoning was good as they saw it. The problem was, of course, that an omnipotent and omnipresent God is just as powerful in valleys as on mountains and just as present in Damascus as in Israel. God heard every word they said and he was ticked! His response was clear and prophetic. King Ahab received a prophet only days after the Syrians concluded their secret war council. The prophet's utterance was succinct and powerful: "Thus saith the Lord, Because the Syrians have said, The Lord is God of the hills, but he is not God of the valleys, therefore will I deliver all this great multitude into thine hand, and ye shall know that I am the Lord" (1 Kgs 20:28).

Obviously God wanted it clear for everyone involved, Syrian and Israeli alike, that he is Lord of all of life, the valleys no less than the hills. On the mountaintops we are fearful that if we must go down he will not be there, and once there we doubt his presence and power. What courage, hope, and faith is ours when we hear him say, "The Syrians are wrong, and you are wrong if you believe them. I am the God of Valleys."

The Syrian Miscalculation

Western culture, not unlike much of the Western church, has to a large extent bought into what I call "the Syrian Miscalculation." This is the fallacious assumption that God rules in, lives in, and proves himself victorious on mountaintops but we are alone and defenseless in the valleys. Nothing could be further from the truth and God will not lightly suffer us to cherish such a dangerous notion.

Key #1 to Victory in a Valley
Unshackle God

When Ben-hadad and the Syrians invaded the second time, it would have been logical to the natural mind to do again what had already proven successful. Not only is that a surefire way to kill creativity; it is a surefire way to limit God. By demanding that God always do the same thing in the same way we shackle him to our expectations.

To embrace the valleys as well as the mountains is to unchain God. If, in fear of the valley experience, we cower behind walls of insulation that have protected us in the past we may never see his most wonderful victories. The Israeli army left their mountaintop fortress and, willing to experience God in the valley, plunged down upon the Syrians exactly like what they were— the wrath of God.

In the second battle a hundred thousand Syrian infantry were killed in one day by less than ten thousand Israelis. In the face of such slaughter, is it any wonder that Syrian soldiers sought refuge wherever they could? Many fled into the city of Aphek, where a wall collapsed on them and killed twenty-seven thousand more. How do you know if you are having a bad day? Narrowly escape death in battle, take refuge in a city, and have a wall fall on you!

For the people of God it was a total victory, not on a mountain but in a valley. When we hem ourselves up in risk-free comfort we may live a life of ease and miss out on discovering who God is in a valley. The hardest proposition for many modern Christians to accept is that God may ever, for any reason, lead them out of a safe, secure city of refuge and down into a valley of struggle and pain. But unless he does we may grow soft and flabby and lose some of the richest of insights into our Lord, insights which are ours only in valleys.

Unshackle God. Unchain him from your demands for wall-to-wall blessings and embrace the valleys as they come, and come they will. The warp and woof that is sometimes laughter, sometimes tears, sometimes joy, and sometimes grief is not to be feared and rejected. That is authentic life. Mountain to valley to hilltop and down again is the pattern not of unhappy losers, but of life itself.

Once I visited a young minister in the hospital; he had just been told that his right leg had to be amputated. I expected to have to comfort him amid a sea of questions about the rightness of things. Instead I found him embracing the valley with hope and good humor. "Really," he said. "This is great! I always wanted to be the best preacher in this district and I could never make it. Now I think I have a really good shot at being the best one-legged preacher in several states."

Some, in a fierce determination to walk only in blessings, may never know what it is to walk with God in a valley of real pain. God is so good that if an easy chair is all you want from him, he may give it to you. But what a tragedy if, in the name of faith and prosperity, we should miss out entirely on the enriching human experience of a valley of need.

Life, all of it, is a gift of God. How will you know the comfort of his presence in the darkness while you stand in the light? How will you learn what it means that he is husband to the husbandless and father to the fatherless until you weep beside a coffin? Life with all its irregularities is not to be feared, as some do and call it faith, and it is not to be stoically endured, as some do and call it submission. Life is to be lived, mountain peak and valley alike, in the joyful knowledge that an unfettered God is God *of* all and *in* all you experience.

Key #2 to Victory in a Valley
Embrace the Valley of Need

A young preacher sat glumly across the desk from his mentor. The younger man slumped dejectedly on his elbow bemoaning some particular trial of the moment. "I am in a valley this time, the darkest valley I've ever been in."

The elder suddenly leaped to his feet and cried out, "Praise God! Praise God!" Laughing at his young friend's obvious confusion he raced around the desk and tenderly embraced him. "Rejoice, son. Rejoice! Valleys are where lilies bloom!"

A wonderful and oft-ignored truth hidden in its own obviousness is that needs are divinely met only in seasons of need. We limit the miraculous hand of God not so much by a lack of faith as by refusing to allow ourselves to experience need.

Speaking at a missions conference in Alabama, I told of my first bout with African malaria. I recounted how horribly sick I was and how frightening it was to be so ill in a country without medicine. At that time Ghana, where I was, had no Fanzidar or corresponding drugs, not even an aspirin, and the hospitals were useless death traps. Then I shared how one brother knelt by my bed and prayed until I fell deeply asleep. When I awakened I was healed and able to preach that night.

After the service a man in the lobby said just a bit archly, "I heard your story about being healed of malaria. How come that stuff never happens to me?"

Before I could answer, another man said, "You know, Bob, maybe it's 'cause you ain't never caught malaria, which would be real hard to do a settin' here in Alabama."

His point is well-taken. I frequently hear people say they want more miracles, but I always wonder if they are willing to be taken to a place where a miracle is their only hope. "Lord, make me stronger in temptation" necessarily implies going through temptation. "Lord, give me healing miracles in my body" means being in need of one. "Lord, send a financial miracle" is a prayer not answered without a financial need.

The valley of need is the only place that sprouts lilies of grace. Go in. Go on in. Only *in* the valley, not gazing at it, not by avoiding it, and certainly not by fearing it, only *in* the valley will we see the miraculous hand of God.

I always admired the humble, modest, yet unshakable faith of Jim Mann, who introduced me to missions. Once, in the Mexican desert, under a blazing, hot August sun, we broke down on a lonely gravel road miles from the nearest village and many miles from the nearest Pemex station. For a while, we tinkered uselessly with the petulant engine, then drank the last of our water and plunked down under the pathetic "shade" of an almost leafless mesquite.

"I am *so* excited," Jim said at last, not so much to me, I thought, as to the desert oven around us.

"Excited?" I asked, gazing around us. Nothing, not even a lizard, moved in any direction. "About what?"

"About seeing how God is going to handle this." And with that he lay back against a rock and covered his face with his hat.

I struggled against the frustration and resentment slowly rising inside me. How could you deal with such a crazy old coot?

From nowhere, a battered cattle truck suddenly clattered toward us in an impossible cloud of dust. Jim lifted the brim of his hat and peered out casually as though the vehicle was one of hundreds he expected to pass that way.

"Ah," he said. "Here we go."

The cattle truck jolted to a stop beside us, absolutely coating us in baked-on desert dust. From the back jumped a teenaged boy with five or six ancient tools wrapped in a blue bandana. Three men watched silently from the cab. I realized that these four rough-looking hombres could easily have robbed and killed us, but such eventualities never seemed to occur to Jim. The men just stared, however, contemplating how two stupid gringos ever got out there in the first place and why.

Without a word the boy with the tools dived under the hood, disconnected a hose, and blew in it. If he did anything else, I didn't see it. Reconnecting the hose, he muttered, *"Listo"* ("ready") to Jim, who climbed in and tried the key. The engine roared to life, of course, and the boy slammed the hood. Jim raced the engine a couple of times and handed the boy some rumpled peso notes. Our *gracias* acknowledged by an exhausted wave or two from the cab, the boy climbed back aboard and the decrepit vehicle rumbled off in its dust cloud.

"There," Jim said, with just enough condescension to be irritating. "Wasn't that exciting?"

That was a miracle that could only have happened broken down in the middle of a blast furnace. Valleys are what gives life its color, and valleys are where miracles bloom like lilies.

Key #3 to Victory in a Valley
Remember God's Reason

God made known his reasons for the miraculous defeat of the Syrians. "Because the Syrians have said ..." and that "ye shall know...."

God was not upholding the reputation of the prophet who spoke, or of King Ahab, or of Israel as a nation. He was vindicating himself alone. Every miracle is about God's reputation and no one else's. Read the headlines. Evidently the reverse is true as well. God is not nearly as desperate to avoid scandal in the church as we thought he was. Apparently God has made a clear distinction in *his* mind between our reputations and his. We had best keep such a distinction clear in our minds as well. God will vindicate *himself.*

"Because the Syrians have said ..." was the first part of God's reason for giving Israel the victory. God will not, for long, allow his name to be blasphemed. When I survey the devastation of post-Communism Eastern Europe, I must ask myself if it is not

God's answer to their arrogant atheism. "Because the Communists have said...."

The temptation in the West, however, is to think God is endorsing *us*. I remember refereeing a basketball game in which one team failed to show up. When I announced the forfeit, the home stands began to rock with the chant, "Yeah, we win! Yeah, we win!" How amazing, I thought, that they so eagerly took credit for a "win" to which they contributed nothing more than showing up.

When we claim *any* credit for a miracle of God, up to and including accepting it as the Heavenly Housekeeping Seal of Approval on us or our ministry, we forget the reason. In the Middle Ages, Catholics in the hinterlands appealed to Rome for a clear statement of the efficacy of the mass in the light of sinful or fallen priests. In other words, if our priest is keeping a mistress, does it invalidate the power of Holy Communion? In response, Rome formulated the doctrine of *ex opere operato* ("in the operation it operates" or "by the working it works"). The sin of a man cannot nullify the means of grace.

Therein lies an answer for any real miracles of healing under the tent of a bogus evangelist. Why, we ask, would God give an immoral, hypocritical, money-grubbing charlatan a divine miracle? The answer is, he doesn't. Despite the sins of the evangelist, God sees the needs of the hurting and remembers his reason. A healing miracle is not validation of any ministry, or man, or method. *Ex opere operato*.

Ahab is described vividly in 1 Kings 21:25-26. "But there was none like unto Ahab, which did sell himself to work wickedness in the sight of the Lord, whom Jezebel his wife stirred up. And he did very abominably in following idols, according to all things as did the Amorites, whom the Lord cast out before the children of Israel."

Why would God grant victory over Syria to a king at least as wicked as they were? Because this was not about Ahab's name, but God's. When a miracle happens under the hands of the sinful, it proves only the grace of God to them that are in need.

What hope that gives us in our own valleys of need. My faith is not grounded in others, in mastering some confessional or apologetic knowledge, in listening to enough tapes, in getting enough faith, or in doing it "right." My faith is solely in God's vindication of his own name. Any act of grace is not about us, but about God.

With Richard the Lionhearted held hostage on the continent, his young brother, Prince John, ruled England so greedily and autocratically that he became her most hated regent. Hoping that Richard would never see England alive, John allowed his regency to make him arrogant, independent, and rebellious.

It is said that when Richard finally landed secretly in England, a spy brought the word to John in this cryptic form, "The devil is loose." When we seize whatever temporary regency is granted us by heaven and claim any personal ownership over it, we forsake vassalage for outlawry. Then when the rightful king claims his own, it does indeed feel like "the devil is loose."

As you ascend from some deep, deep valley, up toward the higher ground of the victorious, remember the reason. This is not to make you more of a king, but more of a king's servant. When at last the Syrians are destroyed who would have made you a slave, then instantly take that newly won freedom and lay it at his feet whose slave you are.

The Conclusion of the Matter:
"A Valley Full of Stones"

How shall we call the valley in which Ahab's tiny army destroyed the hosts of Syria? Is it a valley of victory? For Israel it was. But for the Syrians it was a place of defeat and destruction. In every valley there are multiple stories and each has its own name. God was, at once, dealing with Ben-hadad, Ahab, the prophet, Samaria, Syria, hundreds of thousands of individual soldiers, and all their families.

At the bedside of a dying man in a small southern town I led his grown son to Christ, prayed with his granddaughter to recommit, held his hand as he expired, comforted his wife, and encouraged a nurse whose own father lay dying in another state. We cannot see, from our profoundly limited viewpoint, all that God is working out even as he works on us. The interconnectedness of the stories in a valley are God's tapestry of grace.

Thinking back on one particularly difficult valley in my own life, my family and I sat diagnosing the decisions that had gotten us into it. "Maybe," I offered, "I made a terrible choice in coming here."

"You know, Dad," said my married son. "This may not be about you at all. I mean, what makes you so sure that God brought you here for you? If we hadn't come here I never would have met my wife and he," (indicating my absolutely perfect and gorgeous grandson who is the apple of his grandfather's eye) "*he* never would have been born."

Are you in a valley? Remember that others are there also, and let the God of Valleys glorify his name.

VALLEY OF THE SUN, ARIZONA

Descending from more than four thousand feet, snaking past Deadman's Gulch, Horsethief Basin, Bumble Bee, and Bloody Basin, you drive south from Sedona into the Valley of the Sun. At rest areas you study the majestic grandeur of Arizona's moonscape from safe viewing platforms. In your rented Crown Victoria, it is but a cool, comfortable two-hour drive from the rigorous shopping and touristing of Sedona to your hotel and swimming pool in Phoenix. You may dine sumptuously in a world-class restaurant or watch a professional sporting event in one of several gorgeous facilities before retiring to your climate-controlled room. You study the map and tour brochures to decide on tomorrow's adventure. Will you drive up to the Grand Canyon or down to Tombstone to gawk at the O.K. Corral? Ah, well, that is tomorrow. Tonight, you sip your diet drink and watch a western on HBO.

The excruciating heat that once hammered settlers now bakes well-oiled tourists. The relentless sun that once intimidated the weak and dared the gold-hungry to risk their lives is now the draw, the source of energetic prosperity.

That rocky valley so forbidding in one epoch becomes, in another, the high-rent oasis of winter-weary Yankees. To the pregnant pioneer staggering behind a wagon in near-delirium from heat exhaustion, the very phrase "Valley of the Sun" must have evoked her every fear. Now the wife of a retired lawyer in Cleveland stamps her boots and, watching the snow melt and pool on the parquet, longs for the week to end. On Friday they'll leave for their condo in the Valley of the Sun.

Two

AIJALON:
THE VALLEY OF MIRACLES

Several of us sat scattered across the lower bleachers, enjoying the sensation of being relaxed and familiar in the presence of a teacher. Gym class over, we lolled in delicious indolence while our coach regaled us with stories of his one year in the minor leagues. To us junior high school boys, it felt like membership in some higher order, inclusion in the inner circle, where teachers—cold, demanding, and distant most of the time—transmogrified themselves into relaxed, jocular human beings.

Coach seemed to like it as well. Soon we were into that easy, masculine banter by which we males awkwardly attempt to accomplish all kinds of highly uncomfortable social tasks such as bonding, dealing with pain, actually talking to one another, and cajoling the shy and reticent into the group experience.

"Hey, Arthur," Coach called to one small, dark lad who seldom spoke. "Do you walk to school or carry your lunch?"

Arthur's baleful brown eyes brimmed with tears, his lip trembled and, without a word, the frail, quiet boy plunged into the locker room. For a second we stared in shock at the locker-room door, then we turned our eyes on Coach. What stunned us more than poor little Arthur's painful panic was the fleeting look of confused hurt on Coach's face. It was like seeing him naked and we quickly looked away. No one would ever mention it, but we had seen it and it would haunt us all our lives.

"Hit the showers!" Coach snarled in his familiar and now comforting growl. "Don't sit around here on your lazy butts all day. Get outta here!"

Like Arthur, we agonize mutely before unanswerable conundrums. Like Coach, we snarl like injured wolves when life and humanity get too complicated. We want simple, clear equations that work every time. Complication is pain and pain is the enemy.

We are a people infatuated by formulae. We have become Sergeant Joe Friday's fan club, wanting only the facts. The most popular books always seem to promise the essential steps, the unbeatable recipe, the immutable laws, or the winning solution. We cannot bear flexibility or complications or intangible variables. We celebrate "cutting to the chase," "getting to the bottom line," and "yes or no answers."

This corrupts and weakens us spiritually as we retreat into oversimplified theological card houses built on teaching tapes with all the answers. We lust for answers, ones that always "work." We want spiritual issues to act like our power windows: push-button controlled, dependable, and under warranty. From church growth to faith healing, we demand the answers in black and white, no nonsense, and without complications.

The problem is that life, truth, God, and folks are exactly that—very complicated. What is more, nothing is more complicated than miracles.

God's Testimony in Joshua 10:1-14

Duped by the Hivites at Gibeon, Joshua and his eldership had made a peace treaty with them to spare them alive. The mighty city of Gibeon became a slave city to Joshua's invading Hebrews. They would hew the wood for the altar of sacrifice and draw water for the Jews, which must have been galling to a once-royal city, but still they were alive and intact, unlike the smoldering ruins of Ai.

Failing to seek counsel and discernment from God, Joshua and his leaders were tricked by the Gibeonite ruse of wearing old clothes and carrying patched wineskins and hard, moldy bread. Such carefully planted evidence gave the Gibeonite delegation the appearance of having traveled from a great distance to seek an alliance with Joshua. This was important because Joshua had made no secret of the fact that he was marching under a divine command to destroy every inhabitant of the Holy Land. If he signed a pact with Gibeon, he violated that order, but if they had told him the truth they would have died and their city would have been burned.

What a strange reception the wily ambassadors must have received when they returned to Gibeon to tell the city that the good news was they would live. Joshua has signed the peace treaty, believing them to be from some far-away land. The bad news was that the inhabitants of their entire city had been made slaves. The cost of life was slavery in Gibeon and the other three Hivite cities.

Three days later Joshua's army marched in to claim absolute dominion over Gibeon, Chephirah, Beeroth, and Kirjath-Jearim, the four cities of the Hivites. The entire population of all four yielded without a murmur, absolutely convinced that God had given the entire Holy Land to Joshua. Slaves or owners, bond or free, the Hivites' only goal was to survive ... and survive they did. Joshua declared the Hivites conquered slaves in an occupied land, but he spared their lives.

Word of this separate peace spread like wildfire among the Amorites. At the invitation of King Adoni-Zedek, a war council of five Amorite kings met at Jerusalem to discuss strategy. Feeling betrayed by the Hivites, this unholy alliance decided first to destroy Gibeon. The plan was to circle west and south, then march north up the Shephelah to the Valley of Aijalon and from the west attack defenseless Gibeon, disarmed by Joshua. Having destroyed Joshua's slaves at Gibeon, the Amorite army, fresh from victory, planned to roll down to Gilgal, where Joshua himself was camped.

By the time this bloodthirsty army reached the Valley of Aijalon, Gibeon's spies knew they were coming and swift riders were sent to Gilgal with a desperate message appealing to Joshua for protection, not as allies but possessions. If we are your slaves, they wrote, then come quickly and defend us. What kind of master allows strangers to slaughter his slaves?

For Joshua the military implications of the fall of Gibeon were at least as important as an ill-informed treaty with slaves. If a massive Amorite army took Gibeon and marched east toward him at the Jordan, Joshua would be fighting uphill all the way. Joshua, always an astute strategist, knew that he must get to the high ground at Gibeon before Adoni-Zedek and the allied Amorites. If he could surprise them there, he stood a chance of driving them back down the western slopes into the valley at Aijalon and south down the Shephelah toward Makkedah.

Time was of the essence and Joshua and his Hebrew guer-
rillas had become masters of the forced march. When the
Amorites attacked Gibeon, expecting to find unarmed and
panic-stricken slaves, they met instead the hardened troops of
Joshua's army. Surprised and out-maneuvered, the Amorites
broke ranks and retreat quickly became rout, with Joshua
attacking ferociously every step of the way. Down toward Beth-
horon, the slaughter at the rear driving them like crazed animals, the Amorites, screaming and shedding armor for speed's
sake, ran praying to their gods for night to hasten.

With Beth-horon in sight the heavens opened—but not with
the answer they craved. A hailstorm of deadly ferocity burst on
them from the northwest with icy stones the size of spearheads.
Helmetless now in order to run, the Amorites found themselves
in a hard rain of death. The first to reach Beth-horon were the
first to die, their skulls shattered by the hail. So many died that
it turned the now-crazed soldiers south toward Aijalon's narrow
valley where, in the open and unprotected, they would be
trapped and destroyed if Joshua caught up with them. Their
one hope was the cover of darkness, and the sun was sinking
fast. Not even Joshua could fight a pitched battle in the dark,
and no god, not even Joshua's, could hold back the night.

From the shoulder of low hills west of Gibeon, Joshua saw
what was happening. Instead of fleeing into Beth-horon, the
Amorite retreat, pummeled by hailstones like sledge hammers,
he veered south into the Valley of Aijalon. From his vantage
point Joshua could see that, if he attacked at full speed south
along the wall of hills east of the village of Aijalon, he could trap
them in the valley and snap the back of the Amorite war
machine. He must not let them out of that valley. He must not.

Turning to the young herald behind him, Joshua was about to command for recall to be blown. Three blasts on the shofar and he could veer his army south and smash the Amorites. But as he turned, his practiced eye estimated the angle of the sun. No time!

In the darkness anything can happen. Your troops can get confused and kill each other, the enemy can melt like wax and pour back over the hills to Makkedah, and men and animals can be seriously injured on unfamiliar terrain.

"Sun!" Joshua cried out and all those near him turned toward their general. "Sun! Stand thou still upon Gibeon; and the Moon, in the Valley of Aijalon!"

They were stunned. Was Joshua actually ordering the sun to cease its relentless march across the heavens so that Joshua, in sunlight, might continue his?

"Shofar!" Joshua cried. "Sound recall and attack. To the south! Into the Valley of Aijalon! There will never again be a day like this one."

Aijalon, Valley of Miracles, was where the sun refused to set.

The Amalekite Miscalculation

The forces of evil always trust in darkness. Darkened minds do dark deeds in dark places. The fallacy in all this, of course, is that the God who spoke light into existence can see in the dark or hold back the night. An all-powerful and all-knowing God whose creativity respects no limits is beyond the comprehension of the Amalekites in Aijalon or at a modern university. Miracles, those magnificent interventions of divine power in the natural order, shattering all our intellectual and theological attempts to limit God, explain him away, or diffuse him in the fog of a pantheon. This is a great truth, that one God almighty made the sun and can make it stand still, turn purple, blink, or do loop-de-loops.

Key #4 to Victory in a Valley
Remember Who God Is

I cut my theological teeth on a noxious mixture of liberalism and dispensationalism, both of which are based on a form of doubt, and both of which cultivate doubt in the life of the believer. Liberalism doubts who God is or ever was, "demythologizing" the miracles of the Bible, and using "higher criticism" to slice away at the arteries of its authority. Liberalism claims that God never parted the Red Sea.

Oddly enough, the dispensationalist who would kill to oppose *that* error, espouses one of his own. Dispensationalism acknowledges, even relishes, biblical miracles *then,* but doubts them *now.* I was taught that signs and wonders and gifts disappeared with the finalization of the Canon. In other words, once the Bible was complete, the God of the Bible changed the way he acts in such a fundamental way as to make himself unrecognizable. A God whose common sphere of operation is the miraculous is quite different from one who has not worked a miracle in nearly two millennia. In that sense, liberalism makes more sense than dispensationalism. At least the liberal believes in an unchanging God: one that has *never* done a miracle. The dispensationalist's God once did them but seems to have forgotten how.

The reasons for our arguments, as I remember those days, were largely based on the reality that we had never seen a documentable miracle, a theology of "inexperience." One thing I have learned is that just because the track doesn't run past your house is no proof that there is no such thing as trains. The same God who piled up the waters of the Red Sea, turned the Nile to blood, and spoke his Word into a virgin womb still lives unchanged by either history or bankrupt theologians. Our God is an awesome God—an unceasing, unchanging, undiminished God of miracles.

Miracles are very crucial to who the God of the Bible is. Eliminate miracles and you change the God of the Bible, in which case you may arrive at the untenable theological position of defending an inerrant Bible that reveals a God who has since changed his spots.

On a more personal and practical daily level, we seldom work out our theological positions so finely. Instead we simply forget, in the stress of the moment, who God is. Oh yes, he has been powerful and faithful or even miraculous in the past. But the sun is setting! This situation is different, worse, more difficult, unstoppable. Does the God of Joshua still live? And is he senile?

I received the baptism of the Holy Spirit in 1975, and a universe of fresh possibilities opened for me. I almost immediately saw Scriptures in a new way: as alive, real in the moment, not merely as ancient church history. I had been taught that no one needed to ask for, or could possibly receive, what Peter and John received in the Upper Room. When I did, and in power beyond what I could have imagined, it jolted me into an awareness that, if he could still bestow the Spirit, all my theological givens about God were blasted off the map.

I began to find an almost involuntary interest in physical healing, a topic that had previously held no fascination whatsoever. I established a weekly service of communion and prayers for the sick and, diving into a rich "new" library of faith-stirring books, began to actually see people get better or entirely well. I was intrigued, to say the least, and hungry for more.

Then I entered the Valley of Aijalon, where the needed miracle was my own, and I discovered how quickly we can forget who God is. Stricken with debilitating upper back, neck, and head pain, I finally heard the fearful diagnosis from a local orthopedic clinic. Aggravated degenerative disk disease, the old doctor told me, probably from high school football. I had the worst case he had ever seen in a man under thirty years of age.

"Prepare yourself," he told me. "By the time you're fifty you may well be in a wheelchair. In the meantime we'll try to make you more comfortable."

His idea of "more comfortable" was evidently a medieval torture device akin to the rack. I had to sit for hours a day with a collar around my neck, attached by ropes over the top of a closet door to sandbags on the other side. After two Sunday morning hours of this embarrassing treatment, I was able to go across the street and preach in my church, only to trudge home an hour and a half later in blinding pain.

I learned something in all that. When you see the sun setting on the hills above Aijalon, it's very hard to remember who God is. Frequently we expect, even demand, faith from those least likely to have it, the hurting and demoralized.

Some misbegotten ministerial pride or, more likely, a youthful, inexperienced idea of positive faith kept me from sharing the need with those most likely to pray in faith. At last, however, I broke down at a home cell group of eight elderly ladies and poured out my pain and fear and embarrassment.

They fell on me like crows on carrion. Never, never ever have I been prayed for like I was that night. Like Joshua at Aijalon, they cried out to God, commanded my spine to be healed, threatened the devil, and essentially ordered the sun to stand still. It did! After about fifteen minutes something, with a sound like someone cracking his or her knuckles, went off in my neck. I remember thinking, my God, they've crippled me! But they had not. I stood whole and pain-free, as I remain today, past the age at which that physician prophesied a wheelchair.

I had forgotten who God is but they remembered for me. Joshua had no time to think—no cool, stress-free moment in which to decide who God is. That had to be in him way before Aijalon. That knowledge has to be baked in or it cannot be conjured in the moment of need.

Read about miracles. Collect them like stamps and press them between the pages of your mind. Dig them out of the Bible and rehearse them with people of faith. When your memory slips, get around people of faith. I highly recommend talking with old ladies. Pour faith down inside yourself. The God of Joshua lives and he lives unchanged by all the goofy, faithless theologies in the world.

Key #5 to Victory in a Valley
Listen to God

"And the Lord said unto Joshua, Fear them not: for I have delivered them into thine hand; there shall not a man of them stand before thee" (Jos 10:8).

There is a distinct line between faith and presumption, and it is found in that synapse where *logos* (a general word from God) becomes *rhema* (a specific, personal word from God). There, in the cleft of that rock, we hide from our own pride yet snuggle in, safe from unbelief.

The most strenuous of all theological disciplines is balance. An unbalanced emphasis on personal faith can lead to the dangerous gnostic self-worship that elevates my own faith to the throne and leaves an active God out of the picture. Such an error believes in miracles but puts my hand or tongue on the controls. God forbid! Then there is a false balance that puts hyper-faith on one side of the scales and unbelief on the other. Unbelief does not balance faith; it dilutes it.

The proper balance for faith is the sovereignty of God. Not waiting to hear from God on the matter, many an eager but immature saint has, as Thurber put it, mounted up and ridden off in all directions. The key to Joshua's uncompromised faith at Aijalon was a clear word in Gilgal.

In the early seventies a group of young Korean believers on an evangelistic mission came to a flooded river swollen and impassable with rain. Finding the bridge swept away and claiming by faith the experience of Christ and Peter to walk on water, they plunged in only to be drowned. Their tragic, unnecessary deaths brought reproach on the Korean Christian community.

Some years ago an acquaintance of mine ran for governor of Georgia. Honestly, I didn't know what to think of it and just could *not* seem to hear from God. He finished second in the primaries, forcing a runoff against a popular and better-known candidate. From second to governor came to be an impossible leap and the polls certainly gave no clear indication of the outcome.

On the afternoon of the election, before the polls closed, I heard from God. It seemed to me as clear as if the voice had been audible. He's going to win, it came to me. He's going to win the runoff and the general election because this is my doing and not his. I telephoned his house but he was gone, as you might imagine, to his campaign headquarters to await the start of the returns. I found in his stead his aunt, a godly woman renowned for her faith.

"I know why you've called," she said. "You've heard from God, haven't you?"

"Yes. He's going to win."

"I heard the same thing. He *is* going to win."

And win he did, going on to serve eight years as perhaps Georgia's most popular governor and building a testimony of great Christian leadership that inspired a state.

On another occasion, my song leader of the time, Ronny Brannen, came down with the flu. A friend, Don Martin, and I went to visit Ronny on the way to a revival and, in the brief car trip there, it seemed to me that God's word was clear to me that Ronny would be instantly healed. Interestingly enough, Don acknowledged that he was feeling the same thing.

In Ronny's bedroom we found him looking ill indeed, but I said, with what boldness I could find, though at the sight of him my faith waned, "Ronny, I believe the Lord is going to heal you."

"Well, I hope so," Ronny pouted. "I don't think I'm going to die of the flu."

"No," I laughed. "Not like that. I mean now—right now."

Don and I placed our hands on Ronny's back, which was hot

from fever, and prayed only a few moments. Under our hands Ronny's fever departed instantly.

"That's it," Ronny said, and with that he got dressed and led the singing at that night's revival with, I thought, extreme joy.

Hearing is a key element. It has been my experience and the testimony of many saints that, once you've really heard from God, faith is easy. Until you do, acting precipitously to force God's hand is not faith. It is, however, dangerous.

Key #6 to Victory in a Valley
Obey As Specifically As Possible

Having heard from God that victory was his, Joshua did not wait for it to come to him. He went to it with confident and obedient faith. He obeyed quickly, energetically, and completely. "Joshua therefore came unto them suddenly, and went up from Gilgal all night" (Jos 10:9).

All too frequently, sincere believers, having genuinely heard from God, camp where they are and wait for victory to drop from the sky. Yes, it is possible to race past God, but it is far more likely to sit staring at the sky, as did the disciples at the Ascension.

Go into all the world, Jesus had commanded them, promising to be with them and to return in glory. After he rose through the riven clouds, they stood staring, until God, seeing the problem, sent two angels to break it up.

The promise of victory is usually followed by the command to attack. One wonders, despite having heard from God, what would have happened if Joshua had sat in his seat at Gilgal claiming victory by faith! Victory promised may not come, as long as we sit on our hands. Obedience is the key that unlocks the power of God in the Valley of Aijalon.

In financial stress God may well promise to provide and then command us to take a second job, or sell the car, or move to cheaper digs. We may receive a *rhema* word of deliverance from drugs and alcohol, then be ordered to go into Teen Challenge. There may well come a moment where God, having made a statement to us, wants us to make a statement to him, like leaving Gilgal and making a forced march all night in the dark.

At a Christian businessmen's convention some years ago I shared the platform with another preacher. The meetings had been blessed and altar response strong, but near the end of the last service my colleague felt strongly that someone there had heard a specific word from God and should obey instantly. We urged him to announce this and when he did the wife of a Methodist pastor came running up the aisle weeping loudly.

"I need a miracle in my life," she wailed. "As I was praying, God said, 'You have a diamond ring on your hand that you inherited from your grandmother that is the most important thing in your life to you.' I said, 'No, Lord, you are the most important thing in my life.' And God said, 'Fine, then give the diamond ring away.'"

She said, "I have been fighting God this whole weekend, over what? Over a diamond ring and I'm about to miss my miracle because of not giving this diamond ring away."

She put the diamond ring in the hands of the leader of that convention and said, "Take this and use it for your organization."

Just as she pulled that diamond ring off, the miracle that she was praying for happened. Her Methodist preacher husband came running to the front and stood right beside her and said, "I want to receive the baptism in the Holy Spirit. My wife received the baptism in the Holy Spirit and has been witnessing to me about it, but I couldn't believe it was real until this moment. Now I know it's real. Pray with me."

Suddenly the whole front of the hotel ballroom filled with people weeping, crying, seeking God, and being filled with the Holy Spirit. That preacher's obedience unlocked that woman's, which summoned her husband's, which in turn brought an outpouring of God's Spirit on all of us.

Do not misunderstand. Often the obedience that releases the greatest blessing may be the most demanding in one way or another. One night, while preaching at a Lee University convocation, I felt deeply moved to share my testimony. I had announced a sermon that seemed appropriate to a college audience. My testimony is painful to give and painful to listen to. I have shared it many times in many places and in the book *Launch Out Into the Deep*, but somehow that night airing out my dirty laundry in front of a room full of college kids just galled me. I resisted even until I was in the pulpit.

When, at last, I yielded, it was reluctantly and awkwardly, but God was full of grace to bless it in a marvelous way. The altars filled with students seeking God in deep brokenness, but one young man was worth it all. He came straight to me and surrendered a loaded .38.

"I was in the back row of the balcony," he said, "waiting for service to end and I was going out to my car and shoot myself. Depression has held me all my life. Your testimony has set me free. Take this. I don't need it anymore."

The sun stood still in the Valley of Aijalon. That is a miracle that only the God of the universe could do, but the question remains: if Joshua, having heard the voice of God, had refused to march through the mountains at night, would God still have done it?

The Conclusion of the Matter: "A Valley Full of Miracles"

"When I use a word," the Hatter told Alice, "it means what I want it to mean."

Miracles have come to mean almost anything we want. It's a miracle I made it through the week. It's a miracle that cop didn't give me a ticket. That last touchdown was a miracle. It must have been a miracle; it was a Hail Mary pass. Why, now there is even a women's basketball team in Orlando called the Miracle.

There is, in a way, a justifiable rationale for the broad use of the term *miracle* in a multiplicity of settings. Every baby born is a miracle. The song of a magnolia warbler on a dewy morning in the hills of north Georgia is a miracle. All of the physical order is testimony to the miraculously creative power of God. Used in that sense, we proclaim to the unbelieving world that we see the clear hand of God in the whole realm of nature.

In a more specific sense, however, a true miracle is defined by being that—miraculous. Not merely the wonders of nature or the truly remarkable physical feats of well-trained and talented athletes. I am amazed at what Michael Jordan can do on a basketball court, but it isn't a miracle. Now, if *I* did it, *that* might be a legitimate miracle.

A miracle is the intervention of God *in* the natural order. Water, as beautiful and nourishing as it is, is not properly a miracle. Wine may be the remarkable result of a carefully presided-over fermentation process to produce a highly marketable product, but a miracle it is *not*. If water turns *into* wine, *that* is a miracle.

God is not imprisoned by the physical laws. To perceive him as being such makes him other than he is, which is idolatry. He has created the laws for us so that we do not have to exist in the nightmare of a random universe. If apples fell up we should be holding on for dear life, while everything crashed into everything. God can, however, defy the law of gravity. He can also make molecules of water coalesce to sustain the weight of a human body, cause a severed ear to grow back, make the blind to see, or pluck a golden coin from a fish's mouth.

We must avoid equal and opposite errors. One is denying the miraculous, which is an attempt to make God conform to the shape of our intellect. The other is to arrogantly claim some man-centered theology of miracles that, limiting the sovereignty of God, puts miracles under *my* control.

Christianity is life in the Valley of Miracles, but remember what Joshua said: there will never be another day like this. The sun stood still at Aijalon; that's what makes it a miracle. The sun coming up in glory every morning and setting in splendor on the western hills is marvelous but that "miracle" happens every day. True miracles do *not* happen every day.

We must be slow to shout miracle. If we call everything, anything, too quickly a miracle, we may be, in the eyes of the world, the little church that cried wolf. When the crippled danced for joy, not even the Pharisees could deny "that a notable miracle hath been among us."

Submit to the sovereignty of God, then believe, with all the faith God gives, for the miracle. When it comes, rejoice and humbly give God the glory. When the sun ultimately goes down over Aijalon, which it did, rejoice in a God who can see in the dark.

The greatest miracle I ever saw was a little boy healed, in a single prayer, of a brain tumor. He lay dying, wasted, barely conscious, and gasping for breath when his father, a friend, and I prayed. Never have I prayed with less faith or seen so great a miracle. A child dying in May played Little League in July. A miracle!

I also prayed for a dear friend, a great missionary, to be healed of cancer. I thought I prayed in faith, it *felt* like faith, it was what I usually identify as faith, but he died. Others, many people of great faith, prayed and believed and confessed and claimed and did all we were told was the way to "get a miracle," but he died.

The first did not, in any way, convince me that I have some peculiar access to miracles. The second did not discourage me to pray for a miracle the next time. I live in a valley full of miracles. When the sun stands still in Aijalon, the Lord, he is God. When the sun sinks beneath the purple hills and the Amalekites escape the sword, the Lord, he is God.

VOLTA VALLEY, GHANA

We drove in a Land Rover west from Accra to the foot of a rugged escarpment that boldly announces the Akwapim-Togo Mountains—a range that drapes itself halfway across Ghana. We headed up into the hills and then turned back to the east toward Lake Volta and Akosombo Dam. Ahead of us lay a roughly folded earthen tarp tossed casually like Kente cloth across Ghana's loins.

The deciduous forests there grow rich and thick on the hillsides, and the layered valleys arrange themselves untidily, jutting first in one direction and then in another. Narrow, deep, and teeming with life, these mountain valleys shelter subsistence farms and villages that look much as they did hundreds of years ago. The people here, the Akwapim, speak Twi but with an unusual accent, much as people of remote mountain valleys in Kentucky speak English in their own dialects.

My Ghanaian friend and fellow traveler casually pointed out places of some local interest as we drove. At last he seemed particularly excited. "This is my valley. This is where I was born."

Each man's valley is his own, indistinguishable perhaps to outsiders, but precious and unique to him. "My valley" is a phrase said with deep emotion by none but a native son.

Three

ESCHOL:
THE VALLEY OF
FAITH AND FAILURE

William Wallace, the great Scottish warrior, led a valiant rebellion against an oppressive English occupation of rapine and brutality. With innovation, ingenuity, raw courage, and a brilliant gift for leadership, Wallace enjoyed great success in the field yet died, betrayed and deceived by his own Scottish nobles.

England's King Edward, Longshanks as he was called, experienced nothing but defeat and frustration militarily. Wallace's ragged band of Scottish patriots decimated entire English armies and even invaded England itself, sacking and burning several cities in the north.

What Longshanks could not win in war he gained by knowing human nature. The secret of Edward Longshanks' victory over William Wallace was the devastating power of "the comfort zone." By promising lands and titles to the clan leaders, Edward softened and seduced them into giving up Wallace. Edward knew that they who would rather sacrifice and endure for freedom's sake are a tiny minority compared to the vast host who would ever choose personal advantage without risk. He counted on the Scottish nobility to prefer comfort to battle and compromise to struggle—and he was right.

Wallace, like most brave and noble men, vastly overestimated the courage and nobility of those around him. My own darkest moment in ministry came not because of the opposition of certifiable nutcases, but from the refusal of certain church leaders to take a clear and courageous stand against them. Some spiritual truths, no less than some in the natural realm, cannot be received and truly understood in youth. They are old men's truths, the verities of experience. No one understands why not to touch hot stoves like him with a scarred palm. Not in his passionate youth but in his maturity, King David wrote:

> It was not an enemy ... then I could have borne it: neither was it he that hated me that did magnify himself against me; then I would have hid myself from him: But it was thou, a man mine equal, my guide, and mine acquaintance. We took sweet counsel together, and walked unto the house of God in company.... The words of his mouth were smoother than butter, but war was in his heart: his words were softer than oil, yet were they drawn swords.
>
> PSALM 55:12-21

Comfort is seductive, whether it be a padded chair or just a fear of confrontation. William Wallace found that out. Judas Iscariot chose the comfort of cold cash over sharing the scandal of the cross, betraying his friend with a kiss. David's friend and prayer partner had war in his heart. And in the Valley of Eschol three men discovered the nefarious power of a comfort zone.

God's Testimony in Numbers 13:1-14:45

The blazing desert at their backs, the unsettling, even terrifying experiences of their march from Goshen to Mount Paran behind them, Moses and his refugee army turned their faces, at last, to Canaan. For 430 years the stories of its lushness had graced their firesides. Father to son for more than four centuries, the marvels of Canaan became the ground of their hidden hope, the only thing the Egyptians could not take from them.

Now that they were near its southern border, doubts assailed them. Was it as good as they had been told? No one had actually seen it since the days of Joseph, whose mummified corpse they carried with them. Things often get better in the telling and retelling. Exaggeration, more the fruit of creativity than deception, can inflate anything in half a millennium. To allay their nagging fears and rekindle a longing for their destiny, God had Moses send a squadron of scouts northward into southern Canaan. The Hebrew camp lay in the rugged wilderness called Mount Paran, not really a single mountain as much as a range stretching south from Edom toward the even wider range called Sin.

One man from each tribe was chosen—the best, the valiant, the experienced warriors. This twelve-man detachment of spies headed north, tentatively nudging their way up along the shoulder of hills. Then, growing bolder, the squad pushed on into south-central Canaan even as far north as Hebron.

The prosperity of Canaan was not wasted on men fresh from an extended desert march. They counted herds, estimated flocks, made mental note of vineyards and wheat fields and bulging grain bins. This land was as rich and productive as the legends said.

Skirting the major cities to avoid conflict or detection, they also noted the height of walls and troop movements in and out, while Joshua, always the strategist, pointed out the best attack routes. Caleb alone seemed to enter enthusiastically into such discussions. The others seemed oddly detached, exchanging glances, but Joshua and Caleb put it down to inexperience and uncertainty. It was easy to see how they might feel. They had never before been spies or soldiers or invaders or anything else but slaves and refugees. Now they sat around a campfire plotting the conquest of Canaan. Ah, well, that would pass. Once the invasion began, when these cities fell to them and these lands became theirs, the butterflies would stop. Joshua and Caleb were sure of that.

At Hebron they turned back to the south and, returning by a different route, found a second door back out to Kadesh-barnea, where the gurgling brook Eschol twisted its way down through a small verdant valley fruited lushly and totally without a military garrison. Who would attack from the deserts in the south?

Joshua and Caleb saw it instantly. The Hebrews could pour into Canaan through the Valley of Eschol, being refreshed and strengthened as they came. Plenty of water and grazing and grapes in clusters so massive that the whole valley was named for them: *Eschol* means "cluster."

Hacking away at the vines like gleeful madmen, Joshua and Caleb laughed out loud as they hoisted a pole between them, loaded with grapes, the first fruits of Canaan. The two burden-bearers saw the odd looks on the faces of their fellow scouts. What could it mean?

"Come on, cheer up," Joshua teased them as they marched, the heavy clusters of grapes light on his shoulder. "Do you think that Moses will be mad at us for taking the grapes? We're about to take the whole country!"

The others were silent, refusing to answer.

Caleb thought *he* knew what was wrong. "Are you worried that they won't believe our report? That's it, isn't it? Don't worry. If they don't believe a word we say, they'll have to believe these clusters. If you don't think these grapes will carry weight with the others, then you carry them. Then you'll see how much weight they carry."

But the others refused to be jostled out of their inexplicably sullen mood. Something suddenly seemed wrong. What could it be? Everyone likes to be the bearer of glad tidings.

When the scouts returned, the tumult was as spontaneous and joyful as Joshua had envisioned. Caleb grinned ear-to-ear as he hoisted a massive cluster in each hand and shouted, "Eschols from the Valley of Eschol! The first fruits of Canaan are ours today. Tomorrow, the *rest*!"

"Tell us, Joshua," someone cried. "What our fathers told us—is it true?"

"True? True? The half has not been told. There are so many cattle and goats that the land flows with milk. The blossoms of all that grow there keep a billion bees busy making honey all day. Honey for us!"

"Yes!" shouted Shammual, one of the other scouts, abbreviating the cheer just rising from the camp. "Oh, yes! That is all there. Joshua is telling the truth about that, but it's not the *whole* truth. He's leaving out all the bad news. Does he think we are children to be tricked with stories of cow's milk and beehives? Ask him about the giants!"

Joshua was stunned. "What are you...?"

"That's right!" Palti the Benjamite shouted. "We all saw the richness of Canaan. Tell them the truth, Joshua. Tell of the massive, walled cities with well-equipped soldiers."

This brought a murmur.

"And," screamed Amiel the Danite, *"And* the giants. We *saw* them. We *all* saw them. Joshua and Caleb saw them, too, but they cleverly leave that little tidbit *out,* don't they?"

The murmur grew louder. This was getting out of hand.

Caleb raised his hand for silence, which the crowd begrudgingly granted him. "Yes, they are there. Did you think a conquest was a picnic by the Nile? But we can defeat them all. God is with us. Remember the promise! Remember the...."

"We looked like grasshoppers to them," Sithur interrupted. "Why do you think no one bothered us? Giants do not fear grasshoppers, not even an army of grasshoppers. They just step on them and squash them!"

A woman clutched her baby and shrieked. The clusters of grapes were forgotten. Joyful welcome turned to dangerous disturbance. Aaron nudged Moses backward but, at the movement, someone screamed, "There's Moses. Kill him. Kill 'em all."

"Do what you want. I'm going back to Egypt. There are no giants in Egypt."

"Better a slave than food for giants."

"Our wives will be raped. Our children will be slaughtered and eaten like bread."

At last Joshua blew a shofar and, mounting a rock, spoke in that magnificent voice of his, that voice that led men and stirred souls.

"This land that we scouted is a good land. It *does* flow with milk and honey. Don't listen to these cowards. The *Lord* is with us. We must go in and take it. Where is your faith? Fear is rebellion. God is with us!"

Caleb was certain that this would turn the tide, but he was never more wrong. The seething mob was ready for blood. They were not going in; that much was clear. Screaming for a new captain, they were ready to leave Joshua and Moses *and* Caleb under a pile of rocks and march straight back to Goshen.

This is crazy, Caleb thought. God has given us the land. But he knew it was useless to say any more. The die was cast. One way or another, he had seen the last of the Valley of Eschol.

The Majority Miscalculation

How can so many people be wrong? Very easily! Indeed, it is far more likely that the majority will be wrong than right. This is no assault on the democratic process. It is simply a truth that crowds can become lynch mobs in a flash; the mere fact that the sheriff has law, justice, right, and God on his side is a faint argument to them in their corporate rage.

Once that mob dynamic is unleashed, its ferocious power is virtually unstoppable. In the pursuance of their shared goal, whatever it is, they feel justified—not in the cause alone, but in the very character of the group experience. The bonding power of "us-ness" in opposition to "them-ness" can justify burglary, betrayal, and blasphemy. There is, in group membership, a self-explanation that wipes away even the most obvious moral obstacles, rationalizes anything, and corrupts all reason.

Because a group cannot love (only individuals can love), the group experience demands that love be crucified. A group quickly becomes unreasonable, unentreatable, merciless, remorseless, and dangerous. Almost every ennobling virtue—such as courage, love, faith, and forgiveness—are less likely in groups than in individuals.

The miscalculation of the majority is actually a question. How can "we" be wrong? "We" are united; "we" are agreed; "we" are many; "we" are all members; "we" *must* be right. Weakened by their natural wrong-headedness, individuals within the group at last find it impossible to pull apart and oppose the group.

In a lynching, the mob feels safety in numbers, the shared affirmation of "group-ness," and a stupefying corporate rage that silences any qualms in the individual participants. A writhing, screaming black man, pitiably protesting his innocence, is dragged toward a tree. At the fringe of the mob, a young white man feels a twinge of doubt. Why, that is *Bob* they are going to lynch. I *know* him. He helped me fix my fence and worked hard and faithfully. His wife's name is Ann. Maybe we should wait. What about the law? What about a trial?

Then he gazes about him. He knows these people, too. They could not all be wrong. Could they? Surely not. And if they are all right, then he will be right as well. He is *in*, in the group, *of* the group. He is not some uninitiated outsider uncertain of the rightness of this.

"Lynch him," gurgles up from his own throat and he knows when he hears it that he, *they*, are right.

Moses, Joshua, and Caleb were nearly stoned to death in

the Valley of Eschol. Some who cried against them really wanted to go back to Egypt. Some just wanted to belong.

Key #7 to Victory in a Valley
Don't Overestimate the Enemy

One of the greatest legends of the Texas Rangers concerns a certain Texas trail town that erupted in a dangerous riot, which soon became community war. As the death toll rose and the destruction of private property mounted, the Texas Rangers were telegraphed. "Town in riot. Many dead. Send help."

The answer from Ranger headquarters was comforting indeed, "Help on tomorrow's train."

A brave committee of the town's more respectable citizenry waited anxiously on the platform for the promised contingent of Rangers to arrive and quell the riot. As the few arriving passengers stepped down from the train and scurried off to safety, the citizens' committee waited longingly for sight of the Texas Rangers.

At last, a single, lanky Ranger, his badge obvious against his blue shirt, stepped down from the last car. Their hopes for a quick end to the riot were dashed.

"You're alone?" they wailed. "What can you do? We have a riot here and the Rangers promised help, not one man."

His response is classic Texas rhetoric.

"One riot. One Ranger."

Overestimation of the enemy destroys faith, erodes confidence, and warps perspective. "We were in our own sight as grasshoppers, and so we were in their sight" (Nm 13:33).

In the Valley Eschol, where advance and victory hang in the balance, Satan will rattle his chains, roar like a lion, and generally bang on the pipes if he thinks he can spook you. Fasten your eyes on the size of the challenge and you are already defeated.

Why do you think armies march into battle with banners unfurled and bagpipes blaring? Partly, perhaps, to stir their own troops, but even more to frighten the enemy—to look bigger, braver, and unbeatable. If Satan can get your depth perception far enough out of whack to see yourself as a grasshopper and the problem as gigantic, he has succeeded in crippling your faith. That is Luciferin gamesmanship.

Believers must learn to make it backfire on him like a group of young athletes. While I was in seminary I coached a small inner-city, all-black football team for one season. We had a great season, losing only one game on the way to the "championship" game, of sorts, with another team from an all-white area on the north side of the city.

My team was fleet of foot and eager enough, but they were small and pathetically ragtag. Ill-fitting, tattered uniforms, not all of which even matched, football helmets that looked as if they had come from the Red Grange era, and tennis shoes instead of cleats made us a pretty sad sight. It did not matter when we played teams that looked just like us, but in that final game we came up against a suburban outfit that dressed like Notre Dame.

Their coach had evidently decided to play mental games with my ragged band of gypsies for, when we got to the field, we found his team already there and lined up the width of the parking lot. They were a perfect row of blond heads, matching green jerseys with gold numbers, and gold helmets gleaming like pure ore under each right arm.

"Damon," I shouted at the bus driver, as soon as I saw the situation. "Pull over here and stop, please. Don't go in that parking lot quite yet."

I turned to my rowdy charges and explained, "Gentlemen, look out there. That's no honor guard. They are trying to intimidate you. Look at 'em. Look at those beautiful uniforms. Do you understand what they're saying? They're saying, 'You bunch of ghetto trash, in your torn old uniforms and your tennis shoes, you're not as *good* as we are.' That's what they're saying. I'm not telling you how to respond to them. I just wanted you to understand the situation."

A scream of rage filled that wheezing, yellow school bus and, as one man, they sprang to the side of the bus where that lineup must be passed. Thrusting themselves out to their waists, they began to bang on the side of the bus and chant like cannibals.

"We gonna eat you—uh, uh!!"

"We gonna eat you—uh, uh!!"

"Drive, Damon, drive," I whispered to the driver. "Real slow."

As we drove down the line I watched shoulders slump, fear invade eyes, and lips tremble until I could read their minds. Those boys, for all their fancy uniforms, were already beaten because they were thinking, "They *will*. They will beat us, pulverize us, grind us into powder, and gobble us up."

We later won that game on the field largely because we had already won it in the parking lot. We must learn Satan's tricks. When he stamps around making noise and threats, keep your perspective. He is not a giant and neither, probably, is whatever challenge you are facing. And you are not a grasshopper. You are a child of the most high God with a promise in hand. Go in and take the land. You are well able.

Key #8 to Victory in a Valley
Don't Underestimate God

When he declared his intent to obtain a license to preach, hardly anyone was impressed by the sincere devotion of Buddy Robinson. They were far more sensitive to his barefoot penury (it is said that, at his conversion at nineteen, he had never had a pair of shoes) and his double speech impediment. It was impossible to understand him, let alone imagine him preaching. Yet this illiterate, impoverished, speech-impaired child of moonshiners refused to be deterred. Buddy Robinson's confidence in God so outweighed his more than obvious limitations as to render them moot.

By his death, "Uncle" Buddy Robinson, as he was known, looked back over an expansive ministry that saw him win thousands to Christ as one of the best known and best loved holiness preachers of the early twentieth century. His books (he could neither read nor write at his conversion) have encouraged many, including me, and his story continues to inspire hosts to trust an almighty God.

Talent and intellect are not nearly so important a variable as we think them to be. For sheer victory's sake, I will take the profoundly limited who put no limits on God before the faithless genius whose only hope is in himself.

The Hebrews turned the Valley of Faith into a valley of

failure by underestimating the power of God. Apparently they had no memory for miracles. The plagues, the parting of the sea, and the miracle at Masa all added up to a zero in the face of the giants in Canaan. Do not let the light of yesterday's miracles grow so dim that in today's darkness you underestimate the power of God.

Key #9 to Victory in a Valley
Don't Overestimate the Past

The words *cricket* and *star* do not connect in the minds of modern Americans, but cricket was to nineteenth-century England what basketball is to America. Imagine the explosive effect if a Michael Jordan or a Shaquille O'Neal suddenly announced his conversion to Christ and that he was leaving the NBA for the mission field. That is exactly what happened when the great C.T. Studd retired from cricket for missions.

Born a wealthy aristocrat in Victorian England and blessed with supreme athleticism, Studd became one of the United Kingdom's premier cricket stars. Wealthy, handsome, popular, and athletic, he left it, gave away his substantial fortune, and became instead one of church history's most effective missionaries.

By clinging to the "glories" of the past, whatever we think them to be, we run the risk of missing all that God wants to do in us *now*. The quail and manna at Mount Paran, even life in Egypt, seemed secure and safe compared to fighting giants in Canaan and by comparison looked better than they really were.

The "good old days" have hindered many from hearing

God's call. Don't let your blessings become curses. Fear of letting go of the good can keep you from laying hold of the best.

Key #10 to Victory in a Valley
Don't Underestimate the Future

Keep the vision fresh. Do not allow yourself to be distracted by the challenges you face on the way to receiving the promise. When the Hebrews let the invasion become equated with fighting giants and conquering walled cities, they lost track of the real reason for going through the Valley of Eschol. The goal of the struggle in Canaan was never to defeat the giants but to receive the inheritance of God.

Remind yourself of the reward, rehearse the promise, and refresh the real vision ... or run the risk of losing it altogether in the distractions. One old Florida proverb says, "It is easy to forget your job is to drain the swamp when the gators are nipping at your rear end."

Underestimating the promise can have another unfortunate result: being slow to obey and thereby missing the occasion of God. There is sometimes a limited "window of opportunity" in matters supernatural, and tardy compliance may open us to the dangers of delayed obedience.

When, upon reflection, the Hebrews "changed their minds" and decided to invade Canaan after all, God ordered them not to. They plunged in anyway and the Lord punished them for their presumption by allowing them to lose a terrible battle, a painful and costly lesson indeed (see Nm 14:44-45).

Whenever God calls us to go in through Eschol and take the

land, remember his promises are infinitely sweeter than we can imagine. Lose track of that and lose—period.

The Conclusion of the Matter

In the same valley, one person finds failure, another shows faith. The story for those who failed is brief and bitter: defeat, plague, and death in the desert. For Caleb and Joshua, the reward of their bold faith came forty years later, when they alone, of all of Israel, went in to take The Land.

Consider this remarkable footnote to Caleb's story. Forty years later, when the new generation went in to Canaan, this time from Jericho on the east instead of through Eschol in the south, Caleb claimed a land grant for himself and his people according to God's promise. What he chose was the area of Hebron, the land of giants and the most difficult of all Canaan to conquer.

True adventurers, visionaries such as Caleb, are not just enduring a single struggle for some soft place on the other side. They are inveterate giant killers who seem to have an instinct for challenge. They nose it out. Adventurers head straight for Hebron and the giants, while lightweights look for easy chairs.

THE APALACHICOLA
VALLEY, FLORIDA

The waters of the Apalachicola River that first sprang up somewhere far to the north, probably in the high hills of Georgia, finally slide thick and slow into the Gulf of Mexico. I first saw the
Apalachicola Valley in the late 1950s. It was dozing in the Florida
sunshine: swampy, hot, mosquito infested, and—to me, who had
never seen such—very exotic.

From the nauseating stench of the St. Joe Paper Company to
the rugged poverty of the pathetic fishing village out at the end
of Indian Pass, it was new and exciting and more than slightly
intimidating. Rougher kids than I had ever known soon made me
rougher than I had ever been, until my parents "rescued" us and
moved the family to a kinder, gentler place—suburbia in the
Maryland countryside.

The Apalachicola was in those days, at least, a slow and easy
valley filled with just the sorts of enticements to infatuate a city
kid. It had the "mosquito truck" that rolled through the streets at
dusk spraying behind it a thick, greasy cloud of insecticide; bass-
filled creeks deep in the swamp; and bold-eyed girls from the fish
camp.

Four

SOREK:
THE VALLEY OF SEDUCTION

A handsome Danish prince—well educated, well traveled, and of sterling character—must return home to deal with the untimely death of his father, the king. That is nightmare enough for a college student, but when the ghost of his dead father appears to inform him that it was "murder most foul," young Hamlet is thrust onto the horns of a terrible dilemma that ultimately destroys him.

The classical Greek formula for tragedy is not merely a sad story. A love lost or the death of a child may make a heart-rending, three-hanky movie and still not necessarily, according to the Greeks and to Shakespeare, be a true *tragedy*. A tragedy, *per se,* is the story of a person of high quality, perhaps even of heroic proportions, who is brought to desolation by some flaw in his character. In Hamlet's case it was his inability to resolve the issue of vengeance. Hamlet, a truly fine youth, suffered from tragic indecision, which killed him and almost everyone else in the story. At the close of Hamlet the stage is virtually littered with bodies.

From Macbeth to Willy Loman and from John Candy to Bill Clinton, literature and history offer truly tragic examples of the great and near-great in whom some unresolved inner flaw, like a cancer, brings to grief what promised hope and glory. Among all of Washington's officers none was considered more able than the brilliant General Arnold. He was a fine tactician and a charismatic leader popular with his troops. He had but one glaring flaw. He could not, would not control his spendthrift wife. She literally shopped until he dropped ... right into the arms of the British.

Unable to govern her, he at last became unable to govern himself and yielded to treachery and treason. Benedict Arnold's very name is synonymous with betrayal, but, in fact, he is a tragic figure, the most tragic of the Revolution. Spent into poverty by his wife and spineless in the face of her tirades, a field grade officer who might well have been remembered as second only to Washington, who might have been president himself one day, was brought to shame and infamy by a weakness in his character.

To everyone there comes the dreaded trek through Sorek, the Valley of Seduction. If there is a soft spot in us, Sorek will expose it. Samson was not an evil man, but he was a tragic one.

God's Testimony in Judges 13-16

Samson remembered as he walked. Now he had time for memories. Blind and tied like a mule to a mill wheel in Gaza, he walked, pushed the wheel, and remembered all that had put him there. The pain in his eyes matched the pain in his soul.

That Philistine in Timnath, what was her name? How strange to forget the name of one's first wife. Sloe-eyed and sensual, she reached him in a way that no Jewish girl had ever done. How he had wanted her, ached for her, and now could not recall her name. The lust she had inspired in him at Timnath was as dead as his eyes at Gaza.

He remembered his father and mother pleading with him not to marry a Gentile and his obstinate, childish demands. "Get her for me!" Now that he slept alone in inner darkness on a filthy floor, he remembered his rage when he discovered she had slept with others, his fury with her while she lived, and his vengeance on those who burned her to death.

Tortured thoughts taunted him with all that might have been. The riddle of the lion, how clever he was then, the strength that once had surged within, the laughing lusty thrill of being indestructible. Now just to turn this wheel took all his miserable shred of strength.

In his mind's eye—oh, that they had gouged out that as well—he saw the foxes litter fire like plague across the fields of Timnath. He heard his laughter booming as the creatures yelped and screamed and dragged the torches after them. He saw the bodies of the slain, his victims scattered around like flowers for a bride.

A thousand died before him at Lehi. Samson gripped the handle of the mill wheel, worn smooth by his hands, and remembered the feel of an ass' jawbone rough in his hand and as deadly as any war hammer. There, on the hill at Lehi, the Spirit of the Lord had come upon him—oh, the sensation of that great anointing—and he had slain them like sheep. With a thousand dead at his feet he called the place Ramath-lehi, the Hill of the Jawbone.

He remembered thirst, raging thirst, like the thirst for a woman, consuming him like fire in his veins until he cried out to God, "Shall I now die of thirst, having been given a supernatural victory in battle?"

God heard him that day, heard and cracked the hillside open like a jug till cool spring water gushed out to quench his blazing thirst. En-hakkore, the spring of him who cried to God, became the name of Lehi then. How mighty, how far above the earth he felt to slay a thousand men with nothing but a bone, then name and rename, at his whim, the hills of Israel.

That was En-hakkore then. This lonely, lightless prison house was at Gaza, not En-hakkore. He had been here at Gaza before, not blind and bound and grinding corn, but full of life and lust and power. That prostitute, her name also long forgotten, lived here at Gaza. A night of passion in her arms, a thirst consumed him then as well, only to find himself surrounded by Philistines at daybreak.

What grace, what marvelous grace to receive, in the house of a harlot, the strength to rip away the city's gate and run with them all the way to Hebron. Thirst, it seems, had always warred in him with grace.

From Hebron northwest toward Beth-dagon, heading for the coast, he had to pass through the Valley of Sorek—pleasant, cool, and lush. If only he had gone north or even east into the desert. There in the Valley of Sorek, fresh from the grace of God at Gaza, he saw Delilah dance. Thirst. Oh, God, to never thirst again.

Delilah was the death of him. Worse than death, she was the end of him and God. Dusky Delilah, as lush as the Valley of Sorek, deprived him first of his secret then of his strength and, at last, of everything. His thirst for her had put him here. Can God forgive again?

Awakened in the night, rudely slapped awake, Samson groped along the wall not toward the mill but up along an unfamiliar stair. Was he being released? The hand that led him was that of a child, not sweet and tender, but as a child might tug a reluctant camel.

Noise, voices, the music and laughter of a festival grew louder with each step. He could sense but not see when the corridor disappeared, giving way to a wide expanse and the child's hand dropped away. A moment's silence, then a roar, and Samson knew that he was surrounded by his enemies. Their screams of laughter were sword blows on his soul. Blind and humiliated, Samson became the entertainment for the orgiastic night, groping at thin air and tripping over mere nothings in his way.

He prayed not for life or fame or wealth. Those meant nothing now. The raging thirst is gone too late. Just let me once receive your strength. Let me feel your power as I did at Lehi, Gaza, and Timnath. One final touch of grace was all he asked.

His hand fell upon a pillar. Yes! The surge within—familiar, full of grace and power—rose until he knew exactly what to do. Let God arise and his enemies be scattered. Content to die, but discontent to live without God's touch, Samson put his shoulder to the column and thrust with strength beyond a man's. This, oh this, was his again. At last, one last time and....

The Philistine Miscalculation

The Philistines did *not* miscalculate Samson. They had him figured right enough. They knew that on Delilah's lovely lap the locks of Samson could be shorn. They also knew that, once the secret of his strength was theirs, he was theirs as well. Samson's weakness was not hard to figure out nor his secret to discover. All *that*, they had right.

Who they had wrong was God. The Philistine miscalculation was to underestimate the grace of God. Even as the temple of Dagon imploded on their heads, the Philistines must have been asking themselves, why would God strengthen him now?

Having seen heroes of the faith brought down, the Philistines, whether they carry swords or briefcases, can never imagine a God so gracious as to ever use them again. Gloating from the grandstands, they mock the blinded eyes of yesterday's visionaries and write them off entirely. What could Samson do? Lead him to a pillar. Let him push against it. It comforts the Philistines to have a few scandalized evangelists around. Let them preach. Blind, bald, and utterly forsworn by their God, they are fodder for comedians.

At the Los Angeles Dream Center, I stood in the back of a small, Spartan room and listened to the noon-hour Bible lesson. The "congregation" was a motley crew: the sin-ravaged and road-weary. Ex-prostitutes, ex-pimps, ex-almost everything sat with their Bibles on their laps and listened earnestly to a study of God's Word. The teacher was an "ex" as well, an ex-TV superstar of the Christian world, whose dynasty had boasted multiple studios, a theme park, and a famous hotel. Now he stood in faded jeans and a sweatshirt to teach this tattooed crowd the simple things of God without so much as a microphone.

The Philistines are so wrong, not about us, but about our God. Shorn, blind, and defanged, we, in our weakness, are to be made sport of. We deserve it. But our God is a God of grace beyond the wildest imaginings of remorseless Philistine comedians.

Key #11 to Victory in a Valley
Fight the Real Fight

In all the Bible, perhaps in all of history and literature, there is no more enigmatic and contradictory a character than Samson the judge. He is the prime example of an entire breed of such "men of the flesh" as King Saul, Judah, and Esau. On the one hand Samson was a man of tremendous supernatural strength, able to do great deeds for God, yet utterly unable to control the great wrath and lust that owned him. He was used greatly by God and punished terribly by God; anointed from his birth, yet he died blinded by his own sin.

The tragic flaw in Samson lay in his failure to fight the real battle. The Philistines were not Samson's primary enemy. As Pogo said, "We have seen the enemy and he is us." Samson's carnal nature, at war within himself with the Spirit of power from God, was the real enemy. And Samson never applied his supernatural strength there, where it was most needed.

Samson was emotionally, not spiritually, controlled. Emotionally flawed people are not necessarily those who weep all the time. They are persons whose decisions and judgment are informed more by feeling than spiritual wisdom. Emotionally controlled people cannot be counted on to do what is right but what they *feel* is right at that moment.

Carnality is demanding, self-centered, and unwilling to wait or listen to reason. Samson would not listen to his parents, wait for gratification, forgive an insult, or bend to authority. This is not to say all carnality is sexual. It may be very moral in many ways and even "sound," but its "wisdom" will be earthy, lacking in spirituality, and emotional, not biblical.

A woman I know kept giving money to her drug-addicted son. She bailed him out of jail, paid off his debts, and bought him cars. He, for his part, kept getting arrested, borrowing more money, and wrecking the cars. That he might kill somebody else in a car or himself with an overdose was more practical reality than his mother could handle. When such realities were pointed out, she wailed, "He's my son. You don't understand a mother's feelings!"

The way into the Valley of Sorek is through emotion and appetite. "Get her for me," Samson yelled at his poor beleaguered parents when they resisted his marrying a Gentile. Their weakness and his appetites were a deadly combination. Samson is the quintessential "carnal" man, never able to nail his flesh to the cross and constantly embroiled in some superficial war.

Whomever the carnal believe to be the enemy, the real battle is within. Sensory overload, hyper-emotional decisions, and outward success unmatched by inner strength constitute a recipe for tragic headlines. Satan will happily allow enough outward victory to keep your guard down. He will gladly lose a million battles if he can win the war. Likewise, Satan will send a million outward skirmishes with liberals, in-laws, out-laws, or Philistines if he can keep you from fighting the real war inside yourself.

In the midst of outward battles and outward triumphs, remember that appetite and emotion are the real deal. Pray for the cross to be securely planted in the center of both and believe God for inner victory in the real war.

Key #12 to Victory in a Valley
Seek the Spiritual Above the Religious

It seems remarkable that Samson, in his harlotries, never broke the Nazarite vow of the razor. From his childhood onward his hair never knew a blade. That was only one part, but the most visible part, of the Nazarite lifestyle. Samson was to drink no wine, nor even eat grapes, and keep himself sexually pure. In many ways we find it amazing that he would keep the long hair yet sleep with a prostitute, but that is actually quite typical of the "Samson type" of carnal man.

Spiritually, the deadliest of all combinations is that recipe of carnality and false spirituality called a "religious spirit." King Saul seethed with carnal envy and rebellious disobedience, yet he called on Samuel to pray with him in public and make it "look right" to others (see 1 Sm 15:30). David likewise brought Bathsheba to the palace for an adulterous affair but first made sure she had observed the law to be cleansed from her latest period (see 2 Sm 11:4). Samson kept his hair long like a Nazarite but had sex with Philistine prostitutes like a pagan.

Outward language and mannerisms that roll the religious and the sensual into a single lump must be suspect. Visiting a friend's church, I observed what appeared to be a sensual quality among the praise and worship team. There was an overemotional air to the conversation, and a slightly uncomfortable level of immodesty to the clothing of two of the women.

I was not at all surprised when the pastor told me he was having a "bit of trouble" with the group wanting to "take over" the worship services. Seeing that as an invitation to comment, I mentioned my observation. Later, when the pastor broached the subject with the worship team, however, all hell broke loose in a Scripture-quoting explosion of hurt feelings and counteraccusations.

Within a year, one of the women had an affair, the other went through a divorce, and the worship leader was arrested for fondling a neighbor's child. Worship is intimate, emotional, wonderful, and dangerous. When outward religiosity is not indwelt by inner spirituality it can turn worship into Dr. Feelgood and the traveling medicine show, sending chills down spines and tears down cheeks, yet not reaching the unchecked carnality of the worshipers.

Be real. Refuse to play the spiritual games that so easily coat our gritty humanity with a high-sheen lacquer finish. The longing to sound or look religious does not make us safer; rather, we are even more exposed to temptation and the flesh. To see the carnal impulse for what it is, and rip away its religious camouflage, is a great step toward authenticity.

Some years ago I was co-ministering with Dr. Terry Teykl in a pastor's conference in Texas. One day we lunched with five other ministers attending the conference. Seven preachers in a restaurant have an almost unmistakable air of religion about them, but if the bubbly waitress sensed the sanctity of the gathering she gave no notice.

She was a cute blonde who looked like a million bucks in her little sister's uniform and who said she was just "dee-lighted" to wait on us. When she cocked her hip and batted her big blue eyes, an electric shock went around that table of preachers. "Whatta ya have, boys?" As we ordered far too gruffly, we avoided her eyes and each other's, and when she was gone an uncomfortably awkward silence settled in on the table.

"The Lord has made the heaven and the earth," Dr. Teykl suddenly intoned, to my surprise.

"Hallelujah," our pious chorus responded.

"He made the sea and the fullness thereof." I wondered where he was going with this.

"Praise God," we agreed. "That he did."

"He made humanity as well," Dr. Teykl said with the sweet innocence of St. Francis on his face.

"Hallelujah."

Cutting his eyes at the kitchen door through which our saucy waitress had disappeared, Dr. Teykl said, "He made some pretty amazing humanity, didn't he, boys?"

Instantly the spell was broken, winter was gone, and summer came to Narnia. Pious secrecy plays right into the hands of Satan. Looking straight into another's eyes and admitting our humanity is honesty, and honesty is strength in the Valley of Sorek.

Key #13 to Victory in a Valley
Do Not Confuse Anointing With Permission

One of the more ghoulish pictures of the Middle Ages is Crusader knights killing and plundering in the name of Jesus. Believing themselves to be on so "noble" a quest that any brutality en route was excused, the Crusaders, with crosses on their shields, murdered, and raped thousands on their way to liberate the Holy City from "infidels."

The civil rights leader who grants himself a dispensation for adultery because his greater purpose is so just, the politician whose private sins are acceptable to her because of the glory of her office, or the great preacher who lives in cognitive and spiritual dissonance with what he preaches are all on the same wicked wavelength. Their hope is that the grandness of their vision exonerates the griminess of their sin; the worth of the goal compensates for the warp of the soul.

Samson just could not believe that any man who could slay thousands with a jawbone, rip the city gates off Gaza, and tie torches to fox tails was going to be held accountable for sin in the same way as the unctionless. It is not an uncommon error in the modern church.

I recently counseled with a young man who was struggling with deep hurt and confusion. He had risen through the ranks of the organization of a well-known charismatic evangelist, only to be disillusioned and disoriented. He said that he attended "post-crusade champagne bashes" that got out of hand, even to where one singer on the team was unconscious on the floor. A physician in another state told me that he regularly gave Sunday-morning amphetamine injections to his pastor so that he could preach multiple services "with the power that was expected." And a distraught young woman told my wife she was sleeping with a well-known evangelical teacher after his Bible studies.

What is the problem? Confusion. Victory in battle, success in action, and anointing in ministry feel like cosmic permission not to be held to the same rules as peasants. Stars are different, aren't they?

After every triumph in life or ministry, go quickly to your knees or go slowly into the Valley of Sorek. Anointing has nothing to do with holiness. At the peak of his career David fell with Bathsheba. No person is so important to the kingdom that God will grant private permission to live as others may not.

The Conclusion of the Matter

I stepped from the teeming upbeat intensity of the Christian Booksellers Convention into a pounding gray rain on a deserted Dallas street. A cabby saw me just as I saw him and careened madly across three lanes to the curbside. When I opened the back door I smelled liquor. Not wanting to stand in the rain and hoping it had been spilled on the floor, I edged cautiously in, but I realized in a moment that the driver himself was in grave danger should anyone light a match.

"Sorry, friend," I said, as cheerfully as I could, and stepped back out into the rain. "I'll wait for another cab."

His curses tumbled over each other in angry confusion. "You think you're better than me, doncha?"

"No, I'm not condemning you. Do what you like, but I don't want to die in a Dallas taxicab."

"You were in there, werencha?" he demanded with a slur, jabbing his thumb at the huge sign announcing the CBA. "I used to preach all that. I was once a Baptist preacher in a huge church. Do you believe me?"

"Yes," I said. "I think I do."

"You don't know anything about God that I haven't preached better than you ever will."

With that he screeched away down Commerce Street, ignoring lanes like you would suggestions from a senile aunt. I watched his taillights wink and disappear in the deluge and walked the five blocks in the rain. I wished that he *were* a liar, wished that I did not believe him, but something colder and wetter than the rain down my collar told me it was all the truth.

Whatever happened to him can happen to any of us. The Valley of Sorek must be passed through and some Delilah or another will dance until our passions, like a bonfire, flame up to light the night. Be it sex or power or money or a million other Delilahs, they *will* dance. Against their flashing limbs and oh so seductive eyes, our religious games are useless.

Sensual, emotional, deceived, and defenseless, we shall be shorn and blinded by Philistines who love their job. Samson is a symbol of miraculous power in ministry and devastation in the inner person. Only the crucifixion of instinct will win in the Valley of Seduction.

Some years ago at our Youth Advance a boy named Duane got gloriously saved. He was more than saved; he was truly delivered from an inner rage that kept him in fights and threatened his future. At six feet four inches, he was a formidable foe and the others boys feared him with reason.

The first night of the camp he was wonderfully set free. He broke before God, weeping like a baby, then prayed with me for some time. The peace on his countenance was absolutely radiant and, as he lay back in his bunk, I leaned against the wall to soak up a few last minutes with him.

Into that sweet, calm moment a skinny junior high boy with a tumbler full of water sprinted at full tilt. Without hesitation he hurled the contents straight into Duane's face, then realized in horror that he had the wrong room. I braced myself to do all in my power to keep Duane from killing the boy, though in my heart of hearts, I was tempted to walk away.

"Well," I heard Duane chuckle. "I am so tired tonight I believe I can even sleep wet."

With that he turned his face to the wall and I flipped out the light. Duane could have crushed the life out of the mischievous little shrimp but found, instead, a level of victory he had never known before.

Life in the Spirit may sometimes require you to sleep in a wet bunk, but it will spare you scandal and destruction in the Valley of Sorek.

THE BAROSSA VALLEY,
AUSTRALIA

The drive out from Adelaide through the Barossa Valley is a rare pleasure. Mile after mile of gorgeous vineyards grace both sides of the road. I even played tourist, having my picture made under the sign of one of these picturesque wineries—Rutland's.

I have seldom seen such a peaceful and prosperous valley. There was little traffic, attractive homes, and a gentle climate. We had left the children in Adelaide, content to enjoy the novelty of Australian television. My wife kissed me when I told her she was beautiful. There are few valleys I remember more fondly than the Barossa.

Moments like that—fleeting, sweet, and rare—are memories not to be squandered but wrapped in lace and kept in a special place. Everyone needs a place, way back in some locked cabinet of their inner soul, where they keep a cool fall drive up the Barossa Valley. In the heat and craziness of an African airport or in an American board meeting, such a memory can buy you a moment's sanity.

Five

THE VALLEY OF DRY BONES

The terrible burden of the prophet is to see the terrible reality to which others are happily blind. When Jesus descended from the Mount of Olives into a sea of joyful welcomers, he inexplicably burst into tears, crying, "O, Jerusalem!" Everyone else saw the celebration at his arrival; he saw the bloodbath to come.

In A.D. 70, Jesus' awful vision was fulfilled when the Roman General Titus crushed Jerusalem without pity. Flavius Josephus wrote that the blood ran so deep in the streets that the Romans were forced to keep relighting the fires. Everyone else saw the delight of the crowd; Jesus saw their deaths.

We think of prophets as peculiarly blessed, and, in many ways, that is true. In a far more profound way, however, they are peculiarly burdened. Isaiah, Jeremiah, Ezekiel, and others saw the horror as it was to be, and they were rejected.

The prophetic burden of the church in America is to see ourselves as we really are, to see past the prosperity and power and global preeminence to the dry rot. Such a vision of nightmares to come sounds mean-spirited and vicious to people dancing in the streets. Yet the truth must be told. When all America's attempts to compartmentalize its thinking and hide its eyes from the filth prove futile, the prophet must see hope where no one else can.

Mass murder in our high schools, deep racial division, a prurient and embarrassing presidency, and a population too proud and prosperous to be embarrassed are obvious signs of cultural implosion to all but the belligerently blind, who simply refuse to see. Corruption haunts our courts, drugs are so ubiquitous that they flow unchecked from boardroom to ghetto, and sexual immorality is so widespread that we can no longer find our moral definitions. We do not even know what *is* moral, or right or wrong anymore, or apparently even when people are having "sexual relations."

We have had presidents lie to us before, but *before* we cared. Kennedy was no less "out of control" sexually than Clinton, but he hid it from a nation that cared. There have always been homosexual politicians, but they did not use it as a platform for their campaigns. They did not because the nation was not numbed morally by a climate that celebrates "getting away with it" above dignity and honor.

Those so paranoid about the "religious right" trying to "impose" Christianity on America should see what I have seen. They should sit by the bed of a forty-seven-year-old man dying with cirrhosis of the liver while his wife grieves and children despise his name because he has drunk away two businesses and his job and their house and their fortune.

They should stand on the front stoop of a shack that stinks of sin and watch some little five-year-old shaking the last few cornflakes in a dirty bowl, because his mother spent the night with her boyfriend, who lies unconscious on the floor. They should see that little fellow's feet, bare and cold because his daddy shot the money for the heating bill into his arm.

They should see a nine-year-old sell his body on an American street corner to upstanding white, middle-class businessmen in luxury cars. They should see the loneliness, the hurting marriages, the fear, the anxiety, and the hopelessness. They should see three teenaged girls in a wealthy Philadelphia suburb asphyxiate themselves in the garage, should sit at the funeral and watch three sets of beaten, confused parents stare at three white coffins. They should see a thirteen-year-old girl in the finest shopping center in Dallas wearing earrings made of condoms.

We have no choice but to see the bombing of the federal building in Oklahoma City or the carnage at Columbine High School. But too many deny the frayed, tattered fabric of day-to-day devastation—and this they should have to see.

To see all that and know what it could mean for us all is the prophet's burden. The prophet sees past the stock market, past the party, and past murderous celebrities and corrupt politicians seemingly untouchable by impotent civil law. Seeing the looming horror ahead is only half the prophetic task. Then comes another part, the greater part, which is to see past the horror with prophet's eyes and know that our God is still the God of Jesus and Lazarus. This is the God whose best thing is still resurrections. Let us look with one particular prophet's eyes, those of Ezekiel.

God's Testimony in Ezekiel 37

My name is Ezekiel, which means "God will strengthen." May he strengthen me. I was a priest in the land, a happy priest, a priest with a family and a good life in Jerusalem. Now I have nothing. I live in Babylon, my wife is dead, my country is occupied, and my people are slaves.

You say, yes, but God has *called* you as a prophet. What an honor! You are right, but a painful honor, indeed. In Babylon by the River Chebar is no place for a prophet. There among the captives, there among our Gentile conquerors, there I saw my first vision: the glory of God, the cloud of the Shekinah fire enfolding itself over and over again. It was terrifying, beautiful, and glorious all at once. Do not lightly pray for a prophet's eyes.

There in Babylon I saw the rest, unsettling, fierce, and mighty things—like creatures so bizarre that to describe them defies my words, revelations of God, and vision of slaughter that made my skin crawl. Can you understand what it means to *see* your city put to the sword, to *hear* the women scream, and *watch* the temple burned and *know* it all shall come? You cannot begin to comprehend what a terror of the soul it is to sit in Babylon and watch the future desolation of the land, to see the glory leave and not be believed.

In Babylon, I heard from God not for Jerusalem alone, but for the Edomites, Ammonites, and Moabites as well. I *saw* the fall of Tyre and Sidon and *saw* Egyptians scattered like the dust. I *saw* and *saw* and *saw* until my eyes were weary with seeing it all.

My wife died and God commanded me not to mourn. Are prophets not husbands? To be struck dumb. To lie upon my side making siege works in the dirt like a child! Eating defiled bread! Shaving my head and beard! What a joy to wear a prophet's cloak, to have a prophet's eyes. To see until you pray, O Lord, no more.

After all of that, the greatest sight of all, a sight so horrible that it chilled my soul and yet so glorious that it became the turning point. All I saw after that was full of hope, and hope in Babylon, by the River Chebar, is not so easy to find.

The sight was of a valley like none I'd ever seen, so full of bones that, in my vision, I walked as far as I could walk and all I saw was skeletons. Not even skeletons, I should say, because they were so dry that they were disconnected, piled in heaps. They were just bones, a valley filled with bones. Can you imagine how eerie a sight, that vast expanse of bones? No life, no sign of life, not even rotting flesh, but only bones baked by the sun into a dry unending vale of death where life is all forgotten.

"Can these bones live?" God asked me then. What should I say to that? God's questions are his own.

"O, Lord, you alone know the answer to that."

"Prophesy upon these bones," he commanded and his voice filled the valley. "Tell them to hear the word of the Lord."

But what word? Prophesy what? I had spoken death to the living. Now what? Life to the dead?

I mounted a small promontory and, gazing over the valley full of bones, raised my hands and shouted, "Thus saith the Lord God unto these bones, behold I will cause breath to enter into you and ye shall live. And I will lay sinews upon you and will bring flesh upon you and cover you with skin and put breath in you and you shall live; and ye shall know that I am the Lord your God."

How shall I describe what happened next? No human tongue could ever describe the rattle, the tattoo of a million drums that, with a colossal clatter, reassembled bone to bone until a sea of upright skeletons filled the valley floor. Then while I watched—speechless, breathless—upon all these bony frames fully furnished bodies came to be. No man before or since has seen a human host so reassembled bit by bit, before his awestruck, mortal eyes. Sinews stretched, muscles laid in place, and the skin and hair and eyes until they were whole. From shattered, scattered, fleshless, brittle bones to bodies fully formed before my very eyes!

"Now speak again, Prophet," boomed the voice of God. "Speak and summon to this host the Breath of Life again."

I did as I was told and this time called the wind of God to sweep across these bodies, now whole but lifeless in the plain. "Thus saith the Lord," I cried, "From the North, the South, the East, and the West, let the *ruach* of the Lord breathe life upon these slain. Live! Thus saith the Lord, live!"

And live they did! As with one single set of lungs, they inhaled with an audible whoosh, a rushing, mighty wind of resurrection life. A mighty army stood now where only death had been, a conquering host alive in the valley of bones. Not merely bodies formed again in claylike inanimate replication. Life! An army—mighty, strong in its life, and great in power to march before the Lord.

I have seen more than I can tell, more than I wanted to tell. I have seen until I sometimes ached to see no more. But all that I have seen combined cannot compare to life and breath and hope there in the Valley of Bones.

The Babylonian Miscalculation

In bondage, freedom seems unreal, a dream now lost to never come again. The Babylonian miscalculation is to think that Israel, having come to Iraq, shall see Jerusalem no more.

Despair is as devastating as remorselessness. In sin to repent and in punishment to still believe, those are the rails on which ride all the promises of The Land. One ancient rabbinical school held that, when we get to the gates of paradise, the angels will ask, "Did you live with hope?"

To lose hope for ourselves, or for others, is to doubt God. Even as we weep by the River Chebar in Nebuchadnezzar's golden grasp, we miscalculate desperately if we forget that God makes and unmakes kings, returns his people to The Land, and changes empirical degrees by the breath of his nostrils.

Even when we can, somehow, recall God's grace for ourselves, the far more difficult task is to survey the devastation of another's life and hope for him to rise again. I preached in a prison in Georgia one rainy Saturday night in 1976. Among the seekers who answered the altar call was a young man scheduled to be released the next week, scheduled to be reborn from that iron womb, back to the very streets that had once sent him into prison.

He prayed the sinner's prayer with no more apparent passion than the others, looked no more promising in his prison stripes, had no brighter shine in his eyes, and inspired no richer hope in me. His life was a wreckage of sin. He confessed a live-in girl-friend waiting for him to come home, a past of drugs and crime, *and* a great, new hope for his future.

Twenty-two years later at a Bible school in Georgia we met again. Married now to his girlfriend for more than twenty years and serving in the ministry, he had returned for a refresher course in youth ministry. Tall, well dressed, and full of joy, he recognized me immediately and embraced me with delight. The story of the near quarter-century of God's power in his life gushed out to convict me of my lack of faith.

As I left, I felt God challenge me, "Was it him you doubted that night in jail—or *me?*"

Anklebone connect up to da shinbone.
Shinbone connect up to da kneebone.
Kneebone connect up to da thighbone.
Now hear da word a de Lord.

AMERICAN SPIRITUAL

Key #14 to Victory in a Valley
Face Reality

The vision of dry bones was God's revelation of his assessment of the true condition of Israel. Denial was impossible. The divine indictment was clearly correct and horrible. Israel was as dead in its trespasses as a field of bones. What a chilling sight it must have been for Ezekiel: a valley that dwarfed the killing fields of Cambodia.

Many years ago I was the associate pastor of a downtown church in Atlanta. As the old racial barriers began to collapse, first neighborhoods and then institutions began to be integrated, sometimes not all that graciously. One man in our church told me privately that on the day the first blacks showed up he was transferring to a church far out in the suburbs.

"But, Bob," I pleaded, "you are too mature a Christian to let this sin of racism keep a grip on you."

"I ain't no racist!" he protested vehemently. "I work with 'em all week long. Almost all my crew is black. When the weekend comes I do *not* intend to go to church with 'em, but I'm no racist."

Sometimes denial is downright ludicrous. When the diagnosis, to others and to heaven, is not at all obscure, how can *we* be so blind to our own true condition? Because that is part of the pathology of sin itself. Hidden amidst all the leafy abundance of our pretty religious ornamentals lurks the poison ivy of our darkest depravity. Sometimes it is only by a ruthless grace that the covering foliage is pulled away by an omnipotent hand to reveal the reality that we have so desperately denied.

Death is as much in the denial as in the sin itself. After Babylon's first invasion and deportation, the one that took Ezekiel to the River Chebar, life in Jerusalem returned to something like normal. The temple still stood, worship went on unmolested, and business continued as usual.

But it was a mirage, an imitation of life, that denied the obvious historical reality that Babylon could and would gobble up the rest whenever it took a mind to. It also denied the sins of the nation.

> Declare unto them their abominations; that they have committed adultery, and blood is in their hands, and with their idols have they committed adultery, and have also caused their sons, whom they bare unto me, to pass for them through the fire, to devour them.... For when they had slain their children to their idols, then they came the same day into my sanctuary to profane it.
>
> EZEKIEL 23:36-39

How could they sacrifice their children to savage Canaanite deities, then go up to the temple and worship Yahweh? How?

The same way we deny the menagerie of sins in our souls and pray for the lost to be saved. The same way we gossip, lie, and envy and then put our hands up and praise the Lord. The same way we fight all the way to church, speak in tongues in the worship service, and then fight all the way home.

Pray this prayer if you have the nerve. *Lord, open my eyes to see me as you do.*

Key #15 to Victory in a Valley
Remember God's Character

On the steps of a small rural church in Georgia my family and I were observing the obligatory postworship service rituals of southern hospitality, when I overheard my first-grader in conversation with another lad his age.

"My dad has *never* spanked *me,*" the boy bragged.

"Never?" Travis asked incredulously.

"Never!"

I dreaded the ride home. I was just ready to swoop in and retrieve my son from this boastful little Dr. Spockite when Travis' answer came sweeter and truer than any I might have offered.

"Why not? Doesn't he love you?"

Remember, when conviction comes, that God never shows us ourselves because he hates us but because he loves us. The doctor who says it's cancer is *not* the enemy; the cancer is the enemy. Confrontation from God is not contrary to grace. God reveals death in the midst of life expressly *because* he is a God of grace. He loves us too much to let us go on in denial, letting the cancer grow until it's too late. Hard to take? Yes. Hateful? Never!

Many years ago when my elder sister was in high school she started dating a boy of dubious character. When his well-publicized, local reputation as a two-timing womanizer reached my father's ears, he confronted Eve with the story. Ah, the joys of fatherhood. I *now* can empathize in a way that eluded me as I listened to the wailing and gnashing of teeth (my sister's, not my father's) in the living room. You don't want me to be happy! You don't believe *any* boy is right for me! Darrell *used* to be like that, but you don't believe anybody can change!

As my younger brother and I, both of us still in elementary school, pressed our ears to the door listening to these strange and alien teenaged histrionics, we knew two things that we ourselves were to forget in just a few years. But there marveling at our sister's blatant temporary insanity we saw both truths quite clearly.

Dad was right. And Eve should listen to him.

She did *not*, however, until some weeks later when my dad came into the house and said firmly, "Get in the car, Eve. There's something I want to show you."

When they returned moments later from the Dairy Queen, where Dad showed Eve her boyfriend in the tender embrace of a brunette from Apalachicola, the hysteria we had overheard before proved to be mere pre-tremors of the true eruption. Reality is painful to a prom queen.

Dad did not show her that scene in order to hurt her. She learned a tough lesson we all must learn. When your father tells you truths you don't want to hear, remember his true character is of love. A loving dad must sometimes rain the pain of reality upon the reluctant rear end of our denial, but every blow is love in action.

Key #16 to Victory in a Valley
Don't Be Satisfied With Less Than All

There is vast difference between being "not exactly dead" and being fully alive. The resurrection and restoration of skeletons to become fully formed bodies was a miracle of grace. Dust to dust and back to flesh again! Yet silence remained in the valley. No movement, not a single new-formed chest rose and fell; no shout of triumph filled the air. Born again from death's dark grip but halfway there to life in full.

Two kinds of renewal happen on the way to fullness. "Negative" renewal must often come first. Like a fatigued army on a forced march through the desert, we start dropping things unnecessary and too heavy. The drunken husband with a new-born baby in his arms, swears off liquor. The teenaged girl who has been sexually active in high school determines to go to a Christian college and live in purity. Like gas masks and flash-lights, such unwanted items litter the desert floor behind the army advancing toward a better life.

Such a negative phase is negative not because it is bad but because it is about getting the things of death *out*. It is a good phase of renewal and should be gently encouraged. The danger, however, is that, forced to retreat, the army may later pick up items it dropped on the way. Rejoice at the trail of cast-off bur-dens behind you. Shaking off the dust of death must not be taken lightly. But it is not all, is not near enough, and must not be a resting place for long.

"Prophesy to the wind ..." comes the voice of God, a second word for a second work. The absence of death—to reform, to be sincerely born again—must be followed by this breath of life or else our full destiny remains just slightly out of reach. "And the breath came into them, and they lived, and stood up upon their feet, an exceeding great army" (Ez 37:10).

The in-breathed work of the Holy Spirit is crucial—not *a* key but *the* key to moving from redeemed to rescuer. The power to become the alive, mighty, and breathing army of God is in the Holy Ghost. Many sincere believers stop short, missing the full blessing of Pentecost because of a fear of being ungrateful for the first work.

"Salvation was enough for me," one man told me. "If it wasn't enough for you that's *your* problem."

It's *all* our problem because salvation is not "enough," was never intended to be enough. It was not enough for Peter and John and 118 others in the Upper Room, the Samaritans in Acts 8, or the Ephesians in Acts 19; nor is it enough for any Christian who has faced his need for life and power. Salvation will get you to heaven. Death is done to death. The Holy Spirit will make you a mighty army on the way.

The Red Sea parted to let the Hebrews *out* of Egypt, but *out* was not God's final plan. In a precious second work, the Jordan River parted to let them *in*. "Have ye received the Holy Ghost since ye believed?" (Acts 19:2) was Paul's question at Ephesus. Having believed Christ for salvation from death and hell, shall we not now believe him for fullness of life? God forbid!

A clearer model of the subsequent work of grace than here in Ezekiel 37 can hardly be imagined. I am talking about baptism in the Holy Ghost. Every believer saved from death has a destiny in life, the fullness of the Spirit. Don't stop short. Breathe in, and again I say, breathe in. Prophesy to the wind. Call the breath of life into your lungs. Are you born again? Wonderful! The desert of death in the Valley of Dry Bones has no more hold on you. Now prophesy *again.* "Breathe upon these slain, that they may live" (Ez 37:9).

I waited, struggled, wondered what was wrong with me for fourteen long years. Trying, striving, even through seven years in the ministry, but the absence of death would not "make it go." When the Holy Spirit came in fullness, he also came in power and life.

> Breathe O breathe thy loving Spirit
> Into every troubled breast.
> Let us all in Thee inherit,
> Let us find that *second* rest.
> (from "Love Divine, All Love Excelling")

The Conclusion of the Matter

Some years ago I preached the Minneapolis Soul Fest, an annual inner-city evangelistic outreach. From a massive temporary platform we blasted the 'hood with red-hot soul music and the full gospel. At the altar calls, people came forward through the ghetto streets like skeletons rising from the pavement.

One man I'll never forget came forward to stand at the edge of the platform, a woman and small boy at his side. He was a shrunken, emaciated shell of a man, the whites of his eyes as yellow as a lemon, his hands trembling like leaves in a hurricane. After the counselors and some of the pastors had prayed with them, someone called me over and said, "Dr. Rutland, it appears that this man is having a great miracle."

I looked at that man and his hands had quit shaking, the yellow was gone from his eyes, and he was standing calmly. He looked me in the eye and said, "Dr. Rutland, I have been a mainline heroin addict for sixteen years. Something is happening to me. I feel like I am standing up straight for the first time in twenty years. I am going to live for God."

As he seized his wife's hand and started away, the little boy trailing behind him ran back to me.

I said, "What is it, son?"

Pointing to that man, he shouted up to me, "That's my dad!"

I realized that it was the first time in his little life that he had been proud of his father. I thought, "Look at these dry bones. They do walk!"

Ezekiel's vision in the Valley of Dry Bones is hope for America today. Dead in our death and drying in the blistering heat of cultural collapse, we must face reality. But having done that, there is no need for despair. America can still rise and walk. Prophesy! Save us and we shall be saved. Bones be clothed in flesh. Now prophesy again. *Ruach,* wind of God! Heal us and we shall be healed. Breathe on us and we shall live again.

VALLEY FORGE, PENNSYLVANIA

I sit in climate-controlled darkness and view the film before a kindly park ranger hands me a map and points me on my way. It is hot, at least as hot as it gets in Pennsylvania, which is not all that hot for a Texan, but is still worthy of a cold soda pop from the machine. Later I drive down through the park at dusk and watch the deer meander in and out among the trees to gawk at passing cars. They are quite safe and they know it. In Valley Forge, no one shoots anything anymore.

I try, peering up the Schuylkill River Valley, to imagine Washington's men freezing and dying here by the hundreds—twenty-five hundred, in fact—but I cannot quite pull it off. My imagination, which has worked so well for me in so many valleys, somehow cannot conjure cloth-wrapped feet all bloody in the snow. I do not know whether it is the unending stream of cars or the aristocratic, unhurried deer that stare at me with brazen condescension, but I cannot make my mind's eye see Washington kneeling in the snow to seek divine assistance.

It is a funny thing about valleys and history. All that happened in them is not there anymore but is in books and minds and imaginations. What now fills Valley Forge—placid deer and chubby pink tourists with Japanese cameras—are there because once, in a winter of unspeakable agony, men died of smallpox and exposure. Peering out through frozen lashes at snowbound Valley Forge, could those visionary patriots have ever imagined me? Not in a million years.

Six

REPHAIM:
A VALLEY FULL OF ENEMIES

I have heard this same story a thousand times or, at least, enough to be alarmed. It usually goes something like this. Joe Christian hears about a group of Christian businessmen that are launching a diamond mine in South Carolina, so he borrows $100,000 to invest. Then, having spent that prodigious sum in the worthwhile pursuit of proving beyond a shadow of doubt that the only diamonds in South Carolina are in jewelry stores, he now borrows another $100,000 to invest in an oil-well scheme in Israel. He is confident of this because an elder in his brother-in-law's church in Moline has had a "word of knowledge."

Now finding himself $200,000 in debt, his business failing, his wife furious, and his children with little hope of ever going to college, he asks the church for prayer because he is "under Satanic attack." There is a profound difference between being under a satanic attack and being under a stupid attack.

What to do? Look in the mirror and face the truth. Look yourself in the eye and say it out loud, "That was *stupid*, monumentally, titanically, magnificently, unimaginably STUPID. I am not the first man to do something that dumb, and I will not be the last. I am but one in a long line of donkeys that have poured big bucks right down the stupid tube and now I must pay the piper." Now put your hands up beside your head like great, huge ears and bray at the mirror. Hee-haw!

Now then, doesn't that feel better?

That is a wonderful moment. It cleanses the spirit of a man to strip away all that bright and shining cloud of deceit and false spirituality behind which we veil our own sheer idiocy. No one enjoys such a "wonderful moment," but having endured it, you are now in the place where you can find that special divine grace for the stupid and humble that the stupid and proud will never ever know.

I also know a man who was accused of sexual misconduct (it was proven later to be a 100-percent false accusation), then was hit by a drunk driver and hospitalized for weeks, only to have his wife stricken with cancer. While they were both in the hospital, their house burned down!

Now *that's* an attack. Without getting all weird and hyperspiritual, there come those sobering seasons of life when everything you attempt has crumbled to dust, every doorknob has snapped off in your hand, and every tire on all your cars goes flat at once, where you can legitimately say, "This, now *this* is an attack."

Sometimes it is impossible to discern whether it is an orchestrated satanic attack or the occasional pain of living in a fallen universe. All you know is that you are hurting and you cannot really see where you have been all that stupid, at least no more stupid than usual, and it does not matter all that much whether Satan has planned all this or if the variables of life all just dipped at once.

You find yourself crying out to God, at first in agony and

then in anger, horrified at yourself for being so immature and childish. Then at the end of all the spiritual temper tantrums and the railing against divine injustice, broken before God, you quit asking why and begin to find God's grace for what to do. "O, Lord," you pray, "I am in a valley here. I know I've said this before, but not like this. This is a full-blown attack. Their tents are many who seek my soul. I know you are the God of the Valleys, now help me in a valley full of enemies."

God's Testimony in 2 Samuel 5:17-25

What King David did not need now was another attack. His army was depleted from a bloody civil war, exhausted from constant fighting for more than a decade, and only just beginning to breathe easy after running off a superior force of Philistines. He and the whole army needed to rest and refresh themselves. They needed a season of peace in which to become a real nation with a real army and not a loose amalgamation of tribes and fighting units cobbled together into a guerrilla force largely untested by a frontal attack from a real army.

A real army is exactly what the Philistines were. Their tents were spread out across the Valley of Rephaim as far as David's spies could see. They were well-fed, well-trained, well-equipped veterans with no inclination to give David or his fledgling nation time to recover. Furious over being surprised and defeated the last time, they attacked. The Philistines had returned with a massive host filled with blood lust and hot for revenge.

The last time they came, David's bold assault with a lesser force had so shocked them that they had retreated back through the valley and down from the hills of Judah into the lowlands of coastal Philistia. Wisely, David had not pressed his momentary advantage. It is a military mistake to pursue a larger army in retreat with exhausted light cavalry. Instead, David had burned all the heathen idols they had left behind in the valley, confiscated all their abandoned equipment, and returned to Jerusalem. Now, evidently, the Philistines had returned, in full force, to finish what they came for the last time: the destruction of David *and* his infant kingdom.

David lay on his stomach overlooking the Philistine bivouac from a hillside vantage point that afforded him a view of the whole valley. It was not a comforting sight. Years of guerrilla warfare had given David the ability to size up a situation and quickly decide whether to hit and run or just run. He had done plenty of both, and now he and his beleaguered little army were too tired to do either. He studied the faces of the commanders beside him and saw the telltale signs of battle fatigue around their eyes and deep concern etched in every furrowed brow.

David prayed for wisdom, light, help from the God of Israel, but what kind of help could come? There were no reinforcements on the way. He knew his captains hoped he had some new trick up his sleeve and he also knew that he did not. Too weary to think of a plan, David prayed as he seldom had in his life.

As his eyes fell on a grove of mulberry trees to the rear of the main Philistine camp, the familiar, inner Voice came clear. There, David, there is the place from which you are to attack. Move your ragtag army to the shelter of those trees and attack from there when I give you the word.

With his human logic David resisted. But, Lord, what good is that? We are so few that any advantage we might enjoy by attacking from the rear will be momentary. A force this large will wheel around and pin us against the trees. I don't want to be trapped in dense undergrowth.

Attack from there, came the Voice, but wait until *I* give the signal. When you hear the sound of marching in the tops of those mulberry trees, you will know that I have already attacked the Philistines. Come down then, come down into the valley with all your army and I will show you my power.

It was all the plan David needed. Pushing back from the promontory, the king crawled back to where the animals waited with a squire. Squatting in a low circle as military men do to talk of war, David surveyed the haggard faces of his leaders. They needed great confidence—not in David alone but in the Voice of God.

Suddenly David chuckled, low, soft, and conspiratorial as men do who share some private joke at someone else's expense. At this, their eyebrows lifted, but they neither laughed nor joined each other's gaze. They hardly understood their king at all. Indeed, until Saul's death, several of them had fought against him. They did *not* understand but they did believe in him, and they had come to know that warm, confident laugh. When David laughed, his enemies should tremble.

"They're ours," he said at last. "Every one of them, all that we can kill, just like mice in a cat's paw."

"But, Your Majesty…."

"Here we are," David drew in the dirt with a stick. "Here's the Valley of Rephaim. Here, along here, these are those hills over there. Now did you notice that grove of mulberries? There.

Right there. Did you see them? The Lord told me to attack from there."

"How will we...?"

"Tonight," David laughed. "All night. We've marched all night before. We'll filter through these trees. Half there, the other half over here. We'll rejoin at the mulberry grove about dawn and wait."

"Wait, sire? Wait for what?"

"Angels, my dear old friend. Angels."

"Angels, my lord? Did you say angels?"

"I am thirty years old," David announced, standing before them. "I want to see thirty-one, and I will. We all will see the years to come. Because there, right there in those mulberry trees, an army of angels is being assembled. When they attack, *we* attack. This will be great, just great!"

They stared at the young king's ebullient face and barely dared to hope. It could be. He had killed Goliath, eluded Saul, and was king at thirty. Anyway, who had a better plan? David said there were angels in the mulberry trees. Maybe so. They could see no angels. Then again, who knew what David could see?

"When the angels march, we march."

"Yes, Your Majesty. But how will you know *when* the angels march?"

"How would you know from hiding, if the Philistines marched?" David demanded, with a sardonic smile.

"Why, I guess when I heard them. An army that size, attacking in unison, would make quite a noise."

"Right," the king said. "Now, it's almost dark. Soon we start for the trees. Tell your men they must be quiet until the angels move. Then they can make all the racket they like."

"Yes, sire. When the angels march."

"Cheer up. I'll hear them. An army of angels in full attack is pretty loud business."

"Yes, Your Majesty, of course it is."

The Miscalculation of the Mighty

"Hit him while he's down" is among the most pathetic miscalculations of those whose national anthem is "might makes right." Like their father, the devil, the violent and ruthless never know when to quit. They will pound the little guy until he becomes a tiger and torture the worm until it turns. There is great scriptural truth at work in the world: "God resisteth the proud, but giveth grace unto the humble" (Jas 4:6).

The problem with the proud is that they never seem to learn. Some Latin American dictator rapes his own cowed country until they finally rise up and hang him from a lamppost. You might think all the other tyrants in the world would pay attention. Did Milosevic learn from Ceausescu, or Ceausescu from Mussolini? No, they never learn because they continue in one fatal miscalculation: that the Walter Mittys of the world who have never won a round will never, ever find the grace to win the war. The playground bully should read, but then they seldom do, and learn that to attack the meek when they are prostrate upon their own promised inheritance can be pretty risky business.

Key #17 to Victory in a Valley
Be Aware of When Attacks Most Often Come

Some years ago I came down with an affliction called shingles. I use the term "came down" advisedly. I, who have hardly ever been ill, to whom my family refers as the "iron donkey," was hit in the face by a sledgehammer of pain that landed me squarely in bed, taking some absolutely mind-numbing pain medication, for which I think hard-core junkies would do murder.

An "opportunistic disease," my physician called it, which made me think of several former employees, but he assured me it's not the same. Shingles, as I understand it, and remember I am a medical moron, is in the spinal column of everyone who has ever had chicken pox. It cannot manifest, however, that is, *attack* in a painful assault on your sanity, until the body is weakened by some kind of stress such as fatigue or an emotional crisis. Several very strenuous and suicidally scheduled overseas mission trips and an idiotic domestic preaching load had combined enough to weaken my resistance ... and the disease rushed in to make its presence known.

Satanic attack is an "opportunistic disease." It lurks within us and those around us until we, in some weakened condition, fall heir to the manifestation. Be prepared—in marital crises, business turmoil, or an extended visit by your in-laws—to be the subject of such an attack. Lucifer is no gentleman and, seeing you "down in the mouth," he will attempt to cleat you in the face.

The enemy loves to pile on the hassles. It is his favorite tactic. Knowing that the "little foxes spoil the vines," he will release ten of them for every rottweiler he unleashes.

Your car won't start because the battery is dead and, in replacing it, you scrape your knuckles and bleed on your trousers, which you should have changed but didn't because you were in a hurry, and, anyway, how big of a deal is it to change a battery? While changing your trousers, you realize that you are now an hour late for an interview at the local TV station, but you can't call them because your phone is out of order. You start next door to borrow their phone but on the porch you realize that having divested yourself of the bloody trousers, you have failed to replace them with any others, clean or otherwise. Beating a hasty retreat you now discover that you have locked yourself out of the house and must climb through the basement window, cutting your bare knee in the process. When your wife comes home with the groceries, you are eagerly awaiting sympathy and comfort food when she drops a dozen eggs on the porch and screams at you because, somehow, this is obviously your fault.

That, all of it combined, is *not* a satanic attack. It is but the valley. The attack is coming. When the last feather of stress is laid on the brickload of stress until the camel's back is broken, here comes Satan to leap aboard. By expecting his arrival, you will be less frightened when he spreads his tents in the valley of stress.

Satan's second most favorite "opportunity" to attack is in opportunity itself. "When the Philistines heard they had anointed David king over Israel *all* the Philistines came...." Just given a promotion? About to get married? First baby on the way? Brace yourself. Here come the Philistines!

In the face of stress or that "golden opportunity," get hold of who God is and rest on his word of protection. Begin to praise God and calm your spirit as the valley floor fills up with tents.

David—exhausted and fresh from an unendurable civil war that ripped Israel to shreds—saw the Philistines come up to Rephaim. Newly crowned, on the threshold of his greatest glory, he came under the same attack, from the same valley. Opportunistic diseases will choose *any* opportunity, theirs or yours, to attack with a vengeance.

Key #18 to Victory in a Valley
Listen to God and Obey

When you are in a crisis, you think you don't have the time to seek God. Actually you don't have the time *not* to. There is no time that you need to hear from God more than when you are under immediate pressing attack.

With Philistines ranged against him the first time, "David inquired of the Lord" (2 Sm 5:19). That is laudatory to be sure, but, more significantly, when they attacked the second time in the same army in the same valley, David did *not* operate on old orders. "David inquired of the Lord"—again (v. 23).

The most dangerous idea is one that worked once before. God is a God of infinite resourcefulness and will give us wonderfully creative approaches to problem solving if we will only refuse to be trapped in old paradigms. David could easily have reasoned that God, having told him to attack the Philistines "straight up the middle" the first time, would surely call the same play again on second down. Perhaps the Philistines had seen that play and were better prepared the second time. Maybe they had a bigger, better army the second time. And it could be that God just wanted to use angels the second time.

At any rate, God has both hidden information and heavenly agendas that we have not seen. Learning to let God be as creative as he can be is a great key to victory in a valley full of enemies. God told George Mueller, the famous orphanage director in England, to pray for his needs and never ask anyone for money. That's wonderful but it is *not* a law, and making Mueller's story into *your* story may cost you the divine creativity that made both elephants and ants.

Under great duress in a valley full of enemies, David took nothing for granted. He prayed the first time his enemies approached and heard God say to attack immediately. He prayed again, at the second attack, and God said to circle around behind the Philistines and wait.

The old legend of Epaminondas has always amused and intrigued me. Sent to town for butter, Epaminondas brought home nothing but a yellow puddle in the palm of his hand. His mother was furious and told him from now on he was to stop at a certain cold spring on the way home, wrap the butter in leaves and immerse it in the frigid waters until it hardened again. Later, poor Epaminondas went to town for a new puppy and diligently stopped on the way home long enough to drown the pathetic little dog in the spring.

"Lead it behind you on a string," his mother chided him.

The next week, sent to town for a loaf of bread, the lad remembered his mother's instruction and dutifully dragged the bread home behind him on a string. He could not understand why there was nothing left of it when he got home, *nor* why his mother was so angry. Had he not simply done what he was told? Yes, *simply* is the perfect word!

Flexible obedience to the direction of the Holy Spirit is not only a key to true spirituality but an aid to executive success. Great leaders, like David, are sensitive to God's creativity and obedient to his will.

Key #19 to Victory in a Valley
Get God's Timing for His Will

There are two equal and opposite errors that must be avoided in obeying God in a valley of stress, and both are matters of timing. Some hasty souls, having heard from God concerning what to do, race ahead without finding out when. Others, more reticent and cautious, delay obedience until the window of supernatural opportunity is no longer open. Success is nearly as much a result of timing as obedience.

A young man told me that God had revealed to him in a dream that he was to be a crusade evangelist like Billy Graham. He seemed an earnest and sincere youth and nothing about him made me doubt his account. God can and does speak through dreams, and he can and does call young people to evangelism. I did caution the young man to "ponder all these things in his heart" like the Virgin Mary and wait on God's timing.

I saw that my counsel was wasted when he told me that he had rented the Atlanta Civic Center for the next week! My cautions were angrily blown off as unspiritual and needlessly discouraging. I wondered later if he remembered our conversation. The week at the Civic Center started slow and tapered off.

Thirty the first night became zero by the final service in an auditorium that seats thousands, and he was left with the bill. An expensive lesson on timing.

By the same token, there are moments when God calls for immediate obedience and *later* will not do. The late Rev. Al Bruce sat in his pastoral study watching a bulldozer move the dirt around for his church's new parking lot. Prompted by God to go *that moment* and witness to the driver, Al instantly obeyed, but he wondered what the hurry could be.

He climbed up on the bulldozer and boldly presented Christ to the driver, who asked for prayer. Afterward, the Reverend Bruce dismounted, went back into his study, and sat down at his desk. As he did, at that precise moment, the 'dozer tipped over on a steep hillside and killed the driver instantly.

Only at the sound of angels marching in the mulberry trees did David attack the Philistines. Knowing the will of God and being willing to wait for the moment of God, David acted as a successful leader.

There is one caveat. How do you know when God is telling you to "go up against" and when to wait "against the mulberry trees"? There is no substitute for maturity, nothing more maturing than experience, and no way to get experience in a hurry.

A New York cab driver, realizing that his fare was John D. Rockefeller, saw his opportunity to get some priceless financial counsel.

"How can I make good investments?"

"Wise decisions," was the millionaire's succinct counsel.

"Yes, of course," the cabby coaxed. "But how do I make wise decisions?"

"Experience," Rockefeller responded.

"That's helpful," said the hack. "But, how do I get the experience?"

"*Unwise* decisions," Rockefeller explained.

There is no shortcut to learning the sound of marching angels. The prodding of the Spirit, like the internal irresistible "urge to push" of a woman in labor, gives witness that supernatural forces are marshaled. That is the moment of God. Another moment's delay will be rebellion. Then and only then: "Bestir thyself: for then shall the Lord go out before thee, to smite the host of the Philistines" (2 Sm 5:24).

The Conclusion of the Matter

Once I picked up a bedraggled family hitchhiking in a cold Georgia rain. The man and his two little children were some of the dirtiest, wettest people I have ever seen in my life. Before I let them out at the crossroads where they were going one way and I another, they all three, the man and both little children, prayed to receive the Lord. The impulse of my heart was immediately to reach in my pocket and give them some money, but I sensed a caution from the Holy Spirit. "Don't give them anything," he seemed to say. "They have received the Lord. They prayed to receive Christ and if you give them money now it is going to confuse the issue." Feeling that nudge from God, I put my money back in my pocket but it was hard for my emotional self. I did give him my business card on which I wrote the name of a church that I knew about in that town.

Several weeks later I received a phone call from that man. He had gotten a job and a place to live. He and his children had gone to the church I recommended to them and had been baptized.

He said to me, "You know, when I got out of your car I thought you were going to give me some money. When you didn't, I was angry at you. As we walked away in the rain, the Lord spoke to me in my heart. I had been a Christian less than five minutes and I *heard from God.* Do you understand how exciting that was? He said, 'My son, you look to that man for support and this faith that you have found won't work. Look only to me.'"

Less than a month later, I was on a flight from Los Angeles International Airport to the Canton/Akron Airport. On that airplane a young man sat next to me who, in the course of that flight, prayed with me to be saved. Afterward I felt a sudden direction from the Lord to give this young businessman in a suit and a tie whatever money I had in my pocket. This young man was well dressed and he was on an airplane, not a Greyhound bus, and he certainly was not hitchhiking in the rain.

I remembered the family in the rain and hesitated, but the Lord seemed to firmly nudge me to give him all the cash in my pocket. I said, "You know, friend, I wouldn't want to insult you, but now that you've prayed to receive the Lord, I just feel led of the Holy Spirit to give you the money that I have."

I reached in my pocket and found a $20 bill and two or three ones. I said, "Will you accept this money?"

Tears began streaming down his face and he said, "You know, I didn't tell you this because I wanted you to like me. This suit I have on was given to me by a friend. My airplane ticket home to Canton/Akron was paid for by his parents just to get me away from their son. But nobody gave me any money. I haven't had anything to eat and I don't have taxi fare to get home from the airport to my mom and dad's house. After I prayed that prayer with you for Christ to come into my heart, I said, 'All right, God, I have believed you and I thank you for what you've done, but now I'm asking you to provide me with the means to get from the airport to my house.' Now I know God is real."

The sound of the supernatural rustling in the treetops seldom agrees with our physical senses and almost always challenges our natural logic. To attack when caution seems called for or to delay when defeat is imminent is terrifying. But in a Valley of Enemies, under full-fledged attack, learn to listen—listen for the angels.

THE MEKONG VALLEY, VIETNAM

I gazed out across the thick brown waters of the Mekong River at the verdant forest on the other side. Behind that jungled barrier lay Laos; to the north was poor, ravaged Myanmar, and south, down river where the Mekong widens and slows, was Vietnam. Further south was the sea.

Behind me stretched the Golden Triangle of drugs and corruption. Few places in the world have seen as much war, violence, and tragedy as has the Mekong Valley. I couldn't help wondering what could ever bring healing to such a bloody river valley. Poverty as oppressive as the heat has been its curse for thousands of years; now drugs, like the river itself, promises a future as tortured as its past.

Suddenly on the far bank a motion caught my eye, so slight I hardly noticed it at first. A log jutted down into the water, and straddling it was a small boy, his toes in the water. He waved and I returned it with a smile, but there was no way he could have made out my facial features from such a distance.

A frail, near-naked child with his feet in the Mekong waved at the West. I am here, he seemed to say. See me? I am of this valley. I am this valley. I am its past and its future. Over here across the river. Can you reach me?

After a moment he disappeared back into the forest, but I know he's there, older, probably big enough now to carry a gun.

Seven

ACHOR:
THE VALLEY OF TROUBLES

He was an elderly man when he told me the story. Quite elderly, bowed, arthritic, and nearly blind ... but still full of power. It had happened to him eighty years earlier, when he was a small boy in the rough-and-tumble, pre-World War I mountains of North Georgia. But as he told the story, it came alive for me with great impact.

My father was an elder in a holiness church. The preacher there was not like preachers today. He was a hard preacher for hard times. Folks was poor up in them hills, poor and drunk and mean, and my father's preacher preached holiness like he was on fire. When folks heard him preach, they either got right with God or got mad with him.

One that got mad was a local moonshiner. He told ever'body that he was gonna shut that preacher down. That was the wrong thing to do. That preacher got my father 'n me to drive him out to that 'shiner's cabin in our Model T Ford. My father was opposed, figuring that bad man would shoot the preacher, but that old holiness preacher wasn't scared a' no moonshiner with a coon gun. I rode in the backseat. Why they let me go, I'll never know.

When we pulled up in front a' that cabin, the moonshiner, a tall skinny man with a bushy black beard, stepped out on the porch and yelled at us to get outta thar.

"Whoa now," yelled the preacher, climbin' down from our Ford. "I'm the preacher and I come to tell you about Jesus."

The moonshiner stepped off the porch an' thumped that preacher right in the middle of his forehead. Thumped him hard with the heel of his hand an' said, "I know who you are an' I know why you're here. Everybody in these hills is scared of you but I ain't, and I ain't scared a' your God."

That ol' preacher stepped back from that moonshiner, lifted his hands up, an' closed his eyes. He tilted his head back a little an' his voice boomed out like Jeremiah, rolling down the hills like thunder.

"Thus saith the Lord. As you have tapped the man a' God, so shall I tap you."

That's all he said. Then he turned to my father an' said, "Let's go, Purvis. We're finished here."

About two weeks later my father an' me was driving over to Talking Rock when we seen a truck had run off the road purty far down the side of the mountain. My father climbed down to it to see if they was folks hurt that needed help. When he come back up to me, he looked real funny an' he said, "Come with me, son. You need to see this. It's a terrible sight but I don't never want you to forget it."

We climbed all the way down to that truck. It took a good while. My father just about had to carry me, that's how steep it was. Inside that truck was that moonshiner as dead as a stovepipe with the steering column of his truck drove right through his forehead, right where he thumped that ol' holiness preacher. I ain't never forgot that.

Me neither.

The most difficult theological balance for me is between law and grace, judgment and mercy. There seems to be a point beyond which God simply will not be pushed: a line, an invisible, terrifying line that, once stepped over, can never be recrossed. The problem is that, in different lives and for different countries in history, the line seems to move, at least from our profoundly limited point of view.

We know that God is not whimsical. Neither is he to be mocked. When we suffer we cannot help but ask if it is not for our sins. In Job we see that any oversimplified, direct cause-and-effect line between suffering and sin can lead to error, judgmentalism, and sanctimonious arrogance. Still, there's the problem of that moonshiner. I ain't never forgot that.

What can we say to these things? It seems that we *can* say this. There are troubles, valleys full, through which we must walk by faith knowing that they are not there *because* of some hidden sin. Bad things *do* happen to faithful believers. But there are also valleys, like the Valley of Achor, where suffering is because of sin. Usually we can tell which is which by simply searching our hearts in true humility. The Valley of Achor is pain on a plate, a feast of suffering and the option to fast is disallowed.

God's Testimony in Joshua 7

Women seem to weep more pitifully in a wilderness. Screams of grief, howls of loss like the cries of desert foxes pierced the air and hung suspended in the relentless heat. Thirty-six men lay dead at Joshua's feet while their women raged against their widowhood. Thirty-six corpses that seemed to point their lifeless fingers straight at Joshua. What kind of leader was he to let them die in a battle that should have been won without a casualty? How could he have lost so horribly at Ai?

It was a question for which Joshua had no answer. Jericho had fallen before him like a stack of sticks. Ai had no massive walls, no host of mighty warriors. After Jericho, Ai should have been a stroll in the shade. Instead, his men had suddenly showed cowardice, routed in headlong flight back to Joshua, while the archers at Ai dropped nearly half a hundred Hebrew warriors like fleeing, defenseless deer. The sight of those corpses now condemned him from the rocky desert floor, a sight from which he turned and plunged into the Tent of the Presence. Behind him, as the elders fell to their knees and poured dust on their heads, grief and uncertainty gripped the camp like a claw.

Alone in the murkiness of the tent, the air thick with the familiar perfume of incense, away from the wounded, accusing eyes of his people, Joshua let his own emotions show. Seizing the front of his mantle in both massive fists, the great warrior ripped downward and wailed to God, "Why? Why? O Lord God, why did you bring us all this way—forty years in the desert—just to die in defeat? Have you turned your back on us? That's why we turned our backs to the enemy."

Growing calmer, he prayed, "O Lord, if we lose at Ai, the Canaanites will hear about it and gain confidence. Lord, a confident army is harder to defeat. And *you*, Lord? What about you? If we lose, don't you? What about your reputation? Do you want the Canaanites to think you cannot help your people?"

The answer was swift and direct. From out of the cloud, the

Voice came harsh and strong, "Get up! Why are you lying on your face? Israel has sinned. I commanded you to take nothing from Jericho and someone has disobeyed. Stolen loot from Jericho is hidden in his tent and he covers it now with his lies."

"Who, Lord?" Joshua pleaded.

"Get up. Go out and tell the people, one more time, to cleanse themselves of anything from Jericho. They cannot stand up to their enemies with rebellion hidden in their tents."

"But, Lord," Joshua cried out. "What if they do not get it out? What if they still hide it? What should I do then?"

"You know what must be done."

"Yes, Lord."

"In the morning bring them tribe by tribe, household by household, person by person, and I will give you discernment. He who has brought the fire of trouble upon Israel, fire he shall receive."

Outside the Tent of the Presence, Joshua told the people what he had heard. He pled with them to cleanse themselves, not to wait until morning and a confrontation with God.

"If you are taken with the thing, you will be burned," Joshua cried out. "Sanctify yourselves for tomorrow, that's what the Lord said to me. You have until morning."

As the people drifted away to their tents, Joshua turned to his own but he knew there would be no sleep for him this night. He dreaded morning. Surely whoever had taken the loot from Jericho would not risk exposure and death. Surely they knew they could not hide anything from the eyes of God. Surely.

Yet in the morning, as the process of selection began, Joshua sensed immediately that the stolen abomination was still hidden. Insanity. Sheer madness. Judah was the tribe. Surely the culprit could feel the hand of God tightening. Still no one spoke up. The clan of the Zarhites was selected. Tighter. Zabdi's household. Surely not Zabdi. Joshua knew him. No, not him, but in his household. Carmi, Zabdi's son, stepped forward. Not him. Now Achan ... oh, my God ... it's Achan.

Achan's name meant trouble. Oh, God, he had troubled them all. Thirty-six were already dead and now Achan himself, his wife, all his household must be killed. This was a day of trouble for the nation because of a troubled man.

The booty from Jericho was dragged from his tent. Joshua stared at it. A Babylonian robe, some silver coins, and fifty shekels of gold. Would a man die for such as this? Perish for cloth and gold?

Later, after the stoning, after their bodies were burned along with the abominable stuff from Jericho, stones were heaped in a small hill to cover the charred remains. Achan. Had his family foreseen this day? Why else name a child "trouble"?

"From this day on," Joshua told all Israel. "This Valley shall be called Achor. A troubled man has troubled us here."

The Miscalculation of Mischief

The Prodigal Son thinks the money will never run out. His brother rejoices when it does. How odd the miscalculation of mischief that, like the Push-Me-Pull-You, has two heads facing in opposite directions. While the fiesta rages, sinners seldom contemplate tomorrow. They cannot, simply *will* not believe that the piper must ever be paid. Then there is the older brother who can clearly see his sibling's calamitous cir-

cumstances for exactly what they are, the well-earned conse-
quences of sin. But he miscalculates as well. Unable to imagine his brother bouncing back, or perhaps not wishing for him
to, he simply writes him off. Both, thank God, are wrong.

Key #20 to Victory in a Valley
Keep Short Accounts With God

In counseling a couple in deep financial distress, I discovered
that they had $40,000 in credit card debt and had not even paid
their income tax in three years. The federal government was
about to come down on them like Godzilla and their creditors
wanted blood.

"How did you let it get so bad?" I asked.

"We just kept thinking something would happen."

Happen? I thought. What would happen? Maybe they hoped
to catch a leprechaun. Or that a gold train from Fort Knox
would crash on the front lawn. Or Ross Perot would lower
money from his helicopter in the sky. But *nothing* is going to
happen. With that in our minds we will pay off what we can.
Settle the account at the end of each month and carry no balance forward to gather interest like a magnet.

The same is true spiritually. The unconfessed, undealt-with
balance of sin will fester quickly into compound bondage. Sin—
overlaid with shame and guilt that holds us back from going to
the Father to deal with it, energized by a secret determination
to "buy more next month" regardless of the balance, repeated
and strengthened by pleasure's reward—will *quickly* become
bondage.

Settle the account *now*, right this minute, while you can. Drag the filthy stuff out of your tent and expose it to God's eyes. After all, he has seen it already anyway. Confess before confession is useless, repent while repentance will be received, deal with it before God does.

Even at the last minute, God apparently gave Achan time to clear it up. "In the morning ... he that is taken" (vv. 14-15) seems to imply that if, in the course of that awful night, Achan had burned the stolen goods *he* would not have been. This point of view is strengthened when we consider that the indictment on Israel in verses 11-13 is plural, but the punishment is singular. *"They* have sinned ..." *"They* have taken ..." *"They* have put it ..." but *"he* that is taken" in the morning. In other words, there *may* well have been others in that massive camp who did what Achan did but got it *out* of their tents and out of their lives overnight. There *may* have been little fires of repentance all around the camp that night, but not at Achan's tent. His fire would have to wait until morning.

An even more pungent reminder here might be not to ignore warnings. When that couple, so badly in debt, got notices, those were warnings. Every year in April when "income tax" was on everyone's lips and H&R Block ads saturated the airwaves, those were warnings. Achan, as well, was warned but he ignored it.

Everyone has had calls so close that they left us breathless. As young teenagers in Port St. Joe, Florida, some friends and I got hooked on a certain dangerous railroad game. A daily freight train, in order to make one turn, had to slow to a crawl. From a steep embankment, we idiots would leap on, clinging to the side of the clattering train until it turned toward town, allowing us to leap off, at a much higher speed, onto some soft sand dunes beside the tracks.

On one attempt, however, the train seemed to be going much faster than usual as we approached "the dunes." The others gauged it correctly and hit the dunes squarely, albeit a bit harder than usual, but I overshot the mark and found myself hurtling toward a brick wall just beyond the last dune. At the last minute, my foot found the peak of the dune and I dug it in, sending my body, base over apex, down the back of the dune, shaken but unbroken, to rest at the foot of the wall.

"That's it for me," I said to the other boys. "I'm through." I never jumped on or off another moving train.

Now, you may well be thinking how stupid it was to do that the *first* time. I have no defense except temporary insanity, or adolescence, which is the same thing. The point is that at some point you see what the terrible cost of continuing could be and you walk away. If only Achan had heeded the warning....

Key #21 to Victory in a Valley
Count the Cost Carefully

Hidden, undealt-with sin works a terrible double deception. First, it never pays off as much as it promises. The anticipation of the sin, the thought simmering on the hot grill of my inflamed imagination, is always better than the deed itself. The problem is that we continue to fall for the lie rather than believe our own history. *This* time it will be better. It never is quite what we fancied. Why do we keep on hoping for sin to pay off? Here is your brain. *Here* is your brain on lust.

The next deception of sin, however, is far more destructive. Second, sin not only overstates its payoff, it understates its cost. Satan is a sleazy aluminum siding salesman in a plaid suit, overselling his product and burying hidden costs, fees, add-ons, and taxes deep in the small print. Always reckon on the charges being for more than you could ever imagine. Shame, scandal, and embarrassment added on to financial ruin and physical torture are all in that contract somewhere. Read carefully.

It is good to meditate on the goodness of God. Sometimes, however, we need to meditate on the destructiveness of sin. Before you dial that number, or pick up that glass, or go to her embrace, fight the fire of imagination with the fire of imagination. Make your mind's eye see yourself weeping out a gut-wrenching confession to people you love. See the boss firing you, or the police arresting you, or some grim doctor informing you that there is no mistake, you're HIV-positive.

Furthermore, understand that you will *not* pay the costs alone. No one sins in a vacuum. When we sin, someone else always gets hurt in some way. Sometimes it's a stranger. Usually, it's the people we love most.

Again, stoke up your imagination. See the grief and disillusionment in your children's eyes. Imagine your spouse having a nervous breakdown, the spiritual wounds opened in the hearts of your staff or those who believed in you, and the glee of your enemies.

When Achan sinned, his whole family died. This may seem unreasonable, but the possibility exists that they were willing co-conspirators. Those stolen items were hidden in a small tent, not an offshore bank account in the Caymans. Everyone in that tent probably knew all about it.

The Bible is giving us a clear view of the social cost of sin. Play with fire and all those near you may get burned.

This year at our annual Youth Advance, I saw two boys who had come before but now all the telltale signs of deep negative change were there, including sullen expressions, angry eyes, horrid tattoos, and multiple body piercings.

"What *happened* to them?" I asked my son, Travis.

"Their father. When I coached those boys, they were the nicest, most mannerly Christian boys you'd ever want to meet. Last year their father had an affair, divorced their mother, and never even calls them. How to destroy your kids in one easy lesson."

It's one thing when your sin burns *you*. It never ends there, though. In the Valley of Troubles, life touches life. One violent young Achanite can grieve his own parents, infect his girlfriend, slay his victim, leave those parents heartbroken, and cripple a policeman for life. The policeman's wife must go to work, leaving their children as hurting latchkey kids, the younger brother of the slain man becomes so filled with anger that he also does murder, and the HIV-positive girlfriend shares AIDS with five others before she dies.

Sin's devastation spreads out in ever-widening circles of pain. In the Valley of Trouble, even with Achan dead and the rocks piled over his bones, there was confusion and hurt in the hearts of many. Stones and fire will end the sin and punish the guilty, but they do not necessarily stop the hurt for the innocent. President Clinton's Valley of Achor became a nation's pain. The trial is over, but a numb nation waits for healing.

Key #22 to Victory in a Valley
Keep On Reading

The story of Achan would be unbearable if it were the last in the Bible, but it is not even the last in Joshua. Chapter 7 ends, "Wherefore the name of that place was called The valley of Achor (trouble), unto this day" (v. 26, parentheses mine). Keep on reading. In the very next verse God says to Joshua and to us, "Fear not, neither be thou dismayed ... I have given into thy hand the king of Ai, and his people, and his city, and his land."

The sun sets. The sun also rises. We must all pass through the Valley of Trouble, whether we are there because of our sin, someone else's, or just human history, but we dare not dwell there. Life can be a lot longer than we think and the Valley of Achor, no matter how horrible it is, *will* finally end. Keep moving. OK, you failed at Ai before. OK, you staggered through the cleansing firestorm of the Valley of Achor. Now, on to Ai and, this time, to *victory!*

The lead plane that dropped the first bomb on Pearl Harbor was flown by Captain Mitsuo Fuchida. At the end of World War II, having survived the war and the holocaust of two atom bombs, Fuchida surveyed the devastation of his country and was filled with bitterness and hatred for God and for Americans. Surely few men have ever seen their country in so terrible a valley of trouble. Then came the war trials.

Japanese generals and politicians were put on trial for war crimes. Captain Fuchida never denied atrocities had been committed in the Japanese prisoner of war camps, but he maintained that they were also done in American camps. He set out to research and document the action of American soldiers in our prisoner of war camps, mostly here in the United States. In interviewing hundreds of returned Japanese POWs, he found that, instead of telling him what atrocities had been committed against them, they told story after story of how they were treated with dignity and honor.

In a certain POW camp in the American West, a teenage girl visited week after week administering grace, a sensitive word, and a gentle touch. She prayed with the Japanese prisoners, caring for their needs, bringing them packages. The Japanese prisoners reported to Fuchida that, when they asked her why she was doing this, she always answered the same way.

"My parents were missionaries in Japan when the war broke out," she explained. "Because they had a radio transmitter in their house, they were executed as spies, summarily without a trial by your government. They were nothing but missionaries—precious, God-fearing, God-loving missionaries. The sin of your people and the sin of your government has brought trouble upon the world and upon me and upon my family. I felt bitterness, anger, and resentment until God healed me. Now, I am here to heal you."

This story massaged Fuchida's heart until one day in Tokyo he heard an American street preacher share the gospel and gave his life to Christ. From that time until his death only recently, Captain Fuchida became a world-class evangelist, author, and missionary who brought the Lord Jesus Christ to thousands upon thousands in Japan and around the world. The pilot of the lead plane that dropped the first bomb on the first ship to launch the United States into World War II became perhaps that war's greatest trophy of grace.

The Conclusion of the Matter

"Therefore, behold, I will allure her, and bring her into the wilderness, and speak comfortably unto her. And I will give her her vineyards from thence, and the Valley of Achor for a door of hope" (Hos 2:14-15). Six centuries after Achan was stoned to death there, the prophet Hosea makes reference to this obscure valley. He speaks of it not as the gateway to hell but as a "door of hope."

Inching our way through life's most troubled valley, we limp along in unutterable pain. If we could, somehow, by God's great grace, see it as a "door of hope" the Valley of Achor would not hold such terror for us.

I knew a precious young man named Dave whose son, Bobby, suffered from Down's syndrome. One night at a men's meeting, we somehow started sharing the worst and best moments in our lives. Dave said that the worst moment of his life was when Bobby was born with Down's syndrome.

When we asked him what was the best, he said, "The moment when Bobby was born with Down's syndrome."

Are you in a Valley of Unspeakable Trouble and Pain? Let God turn it into a door of hope. Your worst moment may yet prove to be your best.

THE TWEED RIVER
VALLEY, SCOTLAND

A brook, really, more than a river, sparkling and beautiful, the Tweed is as feisty as Scotland itself—joyful and laughing all the way. Scotland is as you have always read it is: the heather on the hillsides, the haggis, and the wet, chilly weather. Scotland always seems to be doing an imitation of itself, but so charmingly, you find it irresistible.

The Valley and the River Tweed have put a word in the vocabulary of clothing, a word known around the world. I stood in a cold Scottish rain and thought how strange that one little valley's invention, a woolen necessity in their weather, has become a luxury for the world.

Eight

THE VALLEY OF DITCHES

The story is told of a certain county in Wyoming that had a sudden scourge of wolves. It seemed that no lamb or calf in the county was safe until, at last, two wolf hunters from Montana were hired. The first morning of their hunt the two wolf killers rolled out of their tent to find themselves completely surrounded by hundreds of ravenous wolves inching closer by the minute.

With the ring of wolves tightening around them, one of the hunters wailed, "We're dead men. Dead men!"

"Are you crazy?" his friend shouted excitedly. "We're rich men! Rich men!"

It seems that the older I get, the more certain I am that true success in life is more about outlook than talent. A more talented painter than Vincent van Gogh can hardly be imagined, but in a dark moment, he cut his own ear off and mailed it to his girlfriend in a shoe box. You just have to feel that his outlook on life was lacking somewhere.

By the same token, evangelist David Ring, a victim of cerebral palsy, might well have yielded to any one of a million "dark moments." His body shaking and weak, his afflicted muscles in radical disobedience, and his speech slurred in a fashion typical of that disorder, I have seen Ring hold congregations of thousands spellbound.

What makes the difference? If it is outlook, can we alter ours? Certainly there are predispositions of temperament that make one naturally more optimistic than another, but the fact remains that there are ways to so redirect our thinking that in a valley of obvious distress we can find successes that others overlook.

One hindering factor that keeps many from a healthy outlook on affliction is the "I deserve this" syndrome. When the roof falls in on us, we can wallow in the rubble *and* in our own self-pity, telling ourselves that this is what we deserve. Getting up or, perhaps, actually fixing the roof seem like acts of rebellion, refusing to "take our medicine like a man."

There are a few things wrong with that. First, let me comfort you with this. Whatever you are going through, you almost certainly *do* deserve it—and *much worse*. But you are *not* going to get what you deserve from God. If everyone got what he or she deserved, the whole world would go to hell. The fact that you "deserve" whatever happened to you does not eliminate the possibility of your finding a blessing in it.

Second, we Americans have largely lost hope for mental discipline in our current obsession with a dismal kind of scientific Calvinism that accepts genetic predispositions as sovereign. From sexual orientation to esthetic tastes, we knuckle under like sheep, muttering, "I am who I am and there is nothing I can do about it."

There is actually much we can "do about it." We can, by God's grace, sort through all the garbage we've been handed by life and refuse to be defined by it. Near my home in Georgia, there is a county landfill. I stopped in there one day to drop off a load of some old metal fencing and struck up a conversation with the attendant.

"Do you like this work?" I asked, fully expecting a sullen, sarcastic "Oh, sure, everybody-loves-working-at-a-landfill" type of answer. Some perverse streak in me just seems to launch into those predictably surly conversations.

Instead, he surprised me. "This here is the neatest, most organized, modern waste facility in Georgia. There ain't no smell, no flies, and no swarm a' circlin' birds. Don't smell nothin', do you? Do you *see* any garbage? No! Well, mister, I'm right proud a' that. From where I stand, that's a good job."

The semiliterate attendant at a tidy landfill who feels a sense of pride in accomplishment is light-years ahead of a college professor who incessantly gripes about his pay, his office, his hours, and his prospects. The difference is not in education, but in attitude.

God's Testimony in 2 Kings 3

The sun was a relentless sledgehammer upon the three kings no less than on their men and animals. Jehoshaphat began to worry that they had made a fatal mistake. Their water skins were empty, and, at the end of seven days of marching, they came, at last, into this little valley east of Kir-Hareseth. They had counted on finding a lush, well-watered valley but found instead a drought-stricken dust bowl. The springs and riverbeds were baked like matzah.

The three kings sat on their horses bravely before the men's eyes, but in whispered tones they discussed the gravity of the situation. The animals would soon begin to die and if the Moabite cavalry swooped down on their horseless armies staggering with dehydration, it would be a slaughter, not a battle.

Jehoshaphat, king of Judah, looked at the other two men, Jehoram of Israel on his right and the Edomite sovereign to his left, and fought against the fear that he was in the wrong place with the wrong people at the wrong time. He wished that he had taken more time to pray about this campaign. It had seemed like a good idea at the time, a way to strengthen diplomatic ties with the two neighboring countries, but now he wasn't so sure.

He thought back over his on-again, off-again relationship with Israel, the Jewish nation on his northern border. An earlier attempt at trying to forge an uneasy alliance with Israel had nearly cost Jehoshaphat his life. He and Ahab, Jehoram's father, had engaged and had been defeated by a substantial Syrian force at Ramoth-Gilead. Ahab had been killed and Jehoshaphat had barely escaped.

After Ahab's death, Ahaziah, his son, took the throne and Jehoshaphat had pulled back a bit. Ahaziah had seemed too aggressive and demanding. In fact, when Ahaziah proposed a maritime cooperation treaty, Jehoshaphat had quickly declined. Something about that trade and commerce agreement had put him off. Later, when childless Ahaziah fell to his death and his brother, Jehoram, had ascended to the throne, Jehoshaphat decided to try again. Wasn't it better for the two Jewish neighbors to be friends than enemies?

Jehoshaphat's decision to make a state marriage between his son and Ahab's daughter, Jehoram's sister, was controversial to be sure, but so far Jehoram had proven a good ally. The young King Jehoram was not as serious about God as Jehoshaphat, not as determined to see a holy people as Jehoshaphat was, *but*

Jehoshaphat was king in Jerusalem, not in Samaria. Let Jehoram run the northern kingdom his own way. Jehoshaphat and Jehoram were in-laws and allies, *not* spouses.

When Jehoram had decided to make a punitive campaign against Moab, he turned quite logically to Jehoshaphat. The Moabites, who had been paying Jehoram substantial tribute for years, had suddenly refused, and the king of Israel had decided to remind them who was in charge. The Edomite king also agreed to join the campaign since three armies are better than one, and it was traditional that allies share the loot. Anyway, you never know when you might need a friend or a favor.

Jehoram had marched south, joining with Jehoshaphat's force at Jerusalem. The two armies then proceeded south, around the tip of the Dead Sea and down to the exotic Edomite capital at Petra. The plan was a bold one, to leave Petra and, circling wide to the east into the desert, attack the Moabites at Kir-Hareseth. With Israel to its west, Moab would never be expecting an assault from the east, out of the desert. The three armies could carry enough water for several days, quickly refill their skins in some well-watered valley on the edge of Moab and attack without warning.

That's where the plan collapsed. They had not counted on drought in Moab. Perhaps, Jehoshaphat thought, if Jehoram had taken the time to find that out he would have seen *why* the Moabites couldn't pay their tribute that year. On the other hand, perhaps he himself should have taken more thought before marching into the desert with an Edomite and a godless Samaritan.

"We're all going to die," Jehoram broke the silence. "The Moabites will find us here with our horses dead and slaughter us like sheep. We're all going to die!"

Jehoshaphat wanted to slap the little coward and tell him to shut up. Instead he said what he should have in Jerusalem, "Summon a prophet. Let's see what God has to say about this."

Jehoshaphat was surprised to learn that Jehoram did not even know that Elisha, the famous prophet from Tishba, was among his followers. Nonetheless, the little bald-headed prophet with fire in his eyes was soon before them.

"Why would you come to me, Jehoram of Israel?" the Tishbite demanded. "Your parents, Ahab and Jezebel, sought guidance from the prophets of Baal. Go to them."

"Please," Jehoram pleaded like a child and Jehoshaphat could barely hide his contempt. "We're all going to die if you don't help us!"

"I will help you," Elisha said, "but not for *your* sake. Jehoshaphat, the king of Judah, is out here in the dry valley with you. Him, the Lord will save. Now bring a minstrel to play while I pray. Let me hear the sweet songs of Zion and not the whining voice of Jezebel's son."

At this Jehoshaphat was relieved beyond words, but when Elisha gave them the Lord's directions, he was amazed. "Thus saith the Lord, without a single drop of rain, without any wind or clouds, the Lord will give you all the water you need for you, your armies, and all your animals. This valley shall run with water. Not only that, you will fill this valley with the bodies of the Moabites. Now dig ditches for the water."

"Ditches, prophet?" asked Jehoram, incredulously. "Ditches for what water?"

"Dig, Samaritan! Dig or die!"

Dig they did. Every time Jehoram or the Edomites wanted

to stop, Jehoshaphat would shout, "More! More ditches! I know you're thirsty. Dig! Keep on digging."

Three armies dug as though their lives depended on it. They literally excavated the little valley and then, exhausted and thirsty, lay on their bedrolls or simply slept where they dropped.

In the night a rainstorm hit the hard red rocks of Edom to the south, overfilled the wadis and became a leaping, crashing flash flood headed north into Moab. By the time it reached the host of sleeping soldiers, it had become a softly spreading lake of water stained bloodred from the Edomite rocks near Petra, oozed silently into the ditches, which filled to the brim as the exhausted soldiers slept.

Not unlike the flash flood from the south, the Moabites alerted to the invasion, marched all night from the north, prepared to attack at first light. Instead, they laughed to see that the allies had slaughtered each other. The valley floor was covered with blood, red in the morning sun, and bodies that lay at random among the pools of gore.

Laying aside their armor and weapons, the Moabites strolled down into the bloody valley unarmed. They needed no swords to strip the dead. They laughed as they came, totally unafraid.

The Moabite Miscalculation

Projection is that emotional device by which we shine upon others, as does a movie projector, some interpretation, motive, or attitude that goes beyond bare fact. Your brother-in-law has kept your lawn mower for two years—*fact*. He's just doing it to get back at you for losing his barbecue apron with Porky Pig on it—*projection.*

The greatest danger in projection, from the leadership perspective, is that it can skew our perceptions so badly that we make disastrous executive decisions based, not on good information, but on highly emotive responses to situations. These responses are in *us* and *not* necessarily in those upon whom we turn our internal projectors. When the Moabites "saw red" in the valley of ditches they jumped to the conclusion that the allies in the valley were as volatile and violent as they themselves. Their "interpretation" of the red liquid on the valley floor was what got them killed.

Remember, when you "see red," wait! Reconnoiter before you waltz into a situation that might be different from what you think. Projecting your own strengths or weaknesses onto others can be dangerous. You only know *what* somebody did. Your louse of a brother-in-law *has* your lawn mower. He has *had* your lawn mower for two years. You may *think* it is because he is meanspirited and vengeful. It may just be because he is lazy and monumentally absentminded.

The Moabites assumed that red meant blood and that must mean a lot of people had died, and that meant treachery in the valley. All they had to do was walk in and pick up the spoils. Projection, the Moabite miscalculation, cost them their lives.

Key #23 to Victory in a Valley
Avoid Bad Partnerships

No man is an island. Good alliances in life can be a source of empowerment and resources for advancement. But bad alliances can be a destructive source of great pain. There are many things that can make for bad "partnerships," and I use the term loosely to mean top staff, high-level employees, and business partners.

Partners with vastly different values and visions, partners with bad morals and bad marriages, and partners whose work ethic is at odds with yours make for long, drought-stricken campaigns. Even partners whose personalities are irritating, despite their helpfulness or even spirituality, can dry up the water in a valley faster than you think.

I always advise engaged or nearly engaged couples to think on these same things. Look past his curly hair; that will fall out one day. Look past her cute little figure. Four babies in eight years can cause that to disappear like flowers in a magic show. Look past those things and see that mildly bothersome, tiny little habit that just barely makes you wince to notice it on a date today. In a dry and barren valley, years from now, when the curly hair and the cute figure are gone with the wind, that habit, that irritating, monstrous huge habit will remain, looming like Mount St. Helens ready to erupt and blow the top off the whole thing. Take the partner, take the habit too. Both may be in your life for a long time.

The worst kind of partnership, of course, is one that is mismatched spiritually. Righteous Jehoshaphat had no business marching off to battle in an alliance with wicked Jehoram. There is a balance, to be sure. This does *not* mean believers dare not ever hire, do business with, or work for unbelievers. I know a man who desperately needed to buy a warehouse, but when a liquor company offered to sell him one, he balked. He asked me if he should buy it.

"*Should* is the wrong word," I told him. "All I can say is that there is no sin in purchasing real estate from the sinful unless you cheat someone else or use it sinfully yourself."

"Yes," he objected. "But what about using my money to prosper them."

"Look," I explained. "We live in a complicated world. You buy groceries at stores that sell liquor. You fly on airplanes that give it away in first class and you stay in hotels that have bars. *In* the world is not the same thing as *of* it."

On the other hand, a deep, close bond in business or a relationship with an unsaved partner is rife with danger. The biblical admonition not to be "unequally yoked together with unbelievers" (2 Cor 6:14) is disregarded at great risk. Be slow to link your destiny in the desert with another destiny uncommitted to the same God you serve.

It is easy to see, of course, why unbelievers want to be in partnership with Christians. They sense, sometimes intuitively, that they also will be blessed for the sake of the righteous. Potiphar and Pharaoh saw that hope in Joseph, Nebuchadnezzar saw it in Daniel, and Jehoram definitely learned it. Jehoram was spared *and* given victory because he was with Jehoshaphat. Jehoshaphat nearly died because he was with Jehoram.

Think hard *and* pray before you sign on the dotted line, say "I do," or take on a partner. Will the ungodly be preserved because of you, or will you be destroyed or just be miserable because of them?

Key #24 to Victory in a Valley
Believe for Grace

You can hear the goofiest stuff. I recently heard a preacher on the radio say that God is not in the business of bailing his children out of their mistakes. Well, *that* about rips the bottom out of *my* boat. His point, I think, was that grace is for sin and not for mistakes, but he tragically overstated his case. Yes, praise his holy name, God *does* bail us out of our mistakes—over and over and over again!

I suppose the risk in making that statement is that spiritual lightweights will presume upon grace, taking no care at all to get guidance, and plunge from one disaster to the next, constantly expecting God to "make it right." But for every one of them, there are millions of the rest of us who get ourselves in fixes every day and do *not* want to be left to our own devices.

Jehoshaphat had made a series of bad decisions: to ally himself with Jehoram and the king of Edom, to march into the desert without enough water, and to enter unfamiliar territory without first gathering intelligence that would have revealed the drought. All those added up to a potentially deadly mistake, yet he still turned to God with the hopeful expectation of guidance and deliverance. If God will redeem us from the pit of deliberate, intentional wickedness, how much more will he rescue us from the pit of stupidity. Let the man on the radio speak for himself. I say, and I say this from vast personal experience, when you find yourself in the Pit of Stupidity, believe for grace and guidance.

One important result of believing for such amazing grace is to keep us from compounding the error. If grace will not reach us on a dry valley floor where all with us may perish, then we must fix it ourselves. Many who will not reach out for grace at the bottom will quickly make the situation worse by attempting to correct mistake with mistake or, even worse, cover sin with sin.

If Jehoshaphat had whirled his army around and attempted to march back to Petra, they would certainly have died in the desert. Attacking the Moabites was hopeless with the horses dying and his army dehydrated. With the Moabites to the north, the Dead Sea to the west, and a vast cruel desert to the east and south, it was time to hear from God.

A young boy, having married in haste, quickly divorces without taking time to hear from God. A pregnant teen compounds one sin with another, killing her unborn child. A senior pastor, having hurriedly hired the youth pastor from hell, acts precipitously to fire him. Every decision and every outcome might be different if we would only believe for grace. You are *not* on your own in this valley; don't act like it.

Key #25 to Victory in a Valley
Prepare for Grace With Faith

Jehoshaphat's ditches were not the victory. They were not even the *cause* of the victory. They were just the vessels to hold all the victory Jehoshaphat was going to get. If he had refused to dig or even dug fewer ditches, the effect of such an outpouring of grace would certainly have been lessened.

The command from Elisha was perfectly clear. "Make this valley full of ditches." *Full* of ditches, doesn't mean one or two here and there, then see what God will do and, perhaps, dig some more. It means *full* of ditches—first. That is the very point where persons *of* faith must lead *in* faith. Surely Jehoshaphat looked at his soldiers and animals dehydrated and fatigued, saw the cloudless sky in the middle of the dry season in the desert near the Dead Sea, and *surely* he sensed his own raging thirst. Faith, only faith, will dig ditches for water that cannot be seen.

If in the driest valley of your life, God says dig, then by all means dig and keep on digging. Don't be stingy. Every time you think that's enough, dig some more. If God says give, give! If he says go, leave! Dream big. Do not wait for the millionaire to walk in and drop the big bucks in your lap before you decide what to build. Blueprints are ditches. A master plan is a valley full of ditches. Dreams are just ditches to receive the grace that rolls down from Edom.

One lady told me, "I don't love my husband anymore and I don't know what to do. I keep on believing God for love but it doesn't come."

"I have the answer for you," I told her. "Fill the valley with ditches. Love is coming but you have no ditches to catch it in. Start telling him you love him. Tell him ten times a day, call him at work, write him love notes. Dig! Tell him he's wonderful, handsome, sexy, and smart. Brag on him, kiss on him, and build him up. You do that for ten years and you will have love in *all* those ditches."

Remember the ditch you dig today will hold the grace you receive tomorrow. If you only dig one ditch, that's all the grace you'll be able to hold. A valley full of ditches is pleasing to the eyes of God. He counts it for faith and delights to fill them *all*.

The next morning, when Jehoshaphat and the three armies

awoke, they saw defenseless Moabites strolling into the valley like sheep begging to be slaughtered. To the amazement of all, when the "battle" was over, if you can call such a lopsided massacre a battle, there was plenty of water for men and horses. While they slept, God filled the ditches. *That* is grace. God may be ready to grant a supernatural outpouring of grace to meet your most desperate need. Faith in action is the key that starts the rain falling in Edom. It will come. Be full of faith. And when it comes, it will so confuse the enemy of your soul that your victory will be far greater and more absolute than you can now imagine.

The wonderful principle of great faith was a central burden of Elisha's ministry. As recounted in 2 Kings 13, Elisha was on his deathbed when another king of Israel, Jehoash, came to beg for one last prophetic word. Elisha told Jehoash to hold a bow in his hands while Elisha, in turn, laid his hands upon the king's. He then ordered the king to shoot an arrow out the window, which Jehoash did. Finally the dying prophet said, "Take the rest of the arrows and hit them on the ground."

The king did it, but only three times. Elisha was furious. "Why didn't you keep on?" he demanded. "Now you will only have three victories. You could have had more!"

Imagine that powerful little prophet rising up from his deathbed to exhort *you,* "Dig! Strike the floor with arrows! Don't stop! Keep on digging!"

The Conclusion of the Matter

Stunned by the initial shock of desperation in the desert, many quit too soon. They never even hear the command to dig ditches because they bail out too quickly.

In 1870, to catch the post–Civil War building boom, three men launched a house and fence paint company. The problem was that dozens of similar ventures started at about the same time and the three men were soon bankrupt. Two of the men quickly had enough and sold their shares in the defunct company to the third for a token amount.

The third man was convinced there was money to be made in paint. He began asking people what would make them buy one brand of paint over another and they all said the same thing. We want to be able to mix and match the colors *we* want and not just use the black or white or green *all* the stores sell.

He took that idea—not paint, but the *idea* for a new way to sell paint—to the bank to ask for financing. The banker declined saying, "Why get the bank involved in this? I'll put up the money—*personally.*" That day those two men, Mr. Sherwin and Mr. Williams, shook hands on a partnership that was destined to cover the earth.

Perhaps you are in a valley now. Maybe you have even caused it yourself. Do *not* quit. It may already be raining in Petra.

THE ANTELOPE VALLEY, CALIFORNIA

Among the sweetest of my childhood memories is tramping about in the desert near where we lived, for a while, in Lancaster, California. On sunbaked, carefree Saturdays, my siblings and I prowled among the yucca plants and Joshua trees in search of arrowheads and buried treasure.

Once we found a part of a wooden wagon wheel and spun endless tales among ourselves of the pioneers who must surely have been its owners. My sister's story was a sad one of a tragic breakdown there in the desert where we found it and of the long-lost graves of those that died there. I imagined a running fight with Apaches and a wheel snapping off in the action, causing the wagon to crash. Only the heroics of the young boy, about my age, saved the family from being scalped.

The best find we ever made was the parched skeleton of a cow. This we trucked in bone-by-bone and loosely "assembled" in a somewhat cowlike pattern on our garage floor. My mother failed to grasp the archeological significance of our work and the whole thing had to be carried back into the desert.

We never found a single antelope in the Antelope Valley, but we did find that cow skeleton. Even today I can see it laid neatly, bone-to-bone, with the cracked skull at its head, on our garage floor. I can also hear my mother's pitiable screech upon finding it. Some people just have no appreciation for science and history.

Nine

SALT AND SUCCOTH: THE VALLEY OF SUCCESS

Billionaire Ted Turner made quite a news splash a few years ago when he announced that he was rewriting the Ten Commandments (not the movie, the Laws), reckoning, I think, that he could do better than the original author. John Lennon said, "The Beatles are bigger than Jesus." That was big news to many of us.

Now, Lennon is gone but Jesus is still here while no one can even remember Ted Turner's big ten. Apparently the danger of success is not just that success makes men arrogant but asinine, as well. Financiers, politicians, athletes, and evangelists seem intent on proving over and over again that pride goes before both destruction *and* idiocy.

History is filled with sublime quotes like the advertisement for the *Titanic* that said, "Not even God can sink the *Titanic*." The Tower of Babel syndrome has sunk more than ocean liners. Not when we are broken and needy, but at the moment of our greatest triumph, we are the most susceptible to the pride that makes fools of the great, and the wanna-bes.

I met a traveller from an antique land
Who said: "Two vast and trunkless legs of stone

155

Stand in the desert. Near them, on the sand,
Half sunk, a shattered visage lies, whose frown,
And wrinkled lip, and sneer of cold command,
Tell that its sculptor well those passions read
Which yet survive, stamped on these lifeless things,
The hand that mocked them and the heart that fed.
And on the pedestal these words appear—
'My name is Ozymandias, king of kings:
Look on my works, ye Mighty, and despair!'
Nothing beside remains. Round the decay
Of that colossal wreck, boundless and bare
The lone and level sands stretch far away."

Percy Shelley, "Ozymandias"

I remember Nikita Khrushchev pounding his shoe on the desk at the United Nations and screaming at America, "We will bury you!" Now the former Soviet Union is in bankrupt ruins and the United States still stands. Among the flood of Eastern European refugees pouring into the United States one tidbit of ironic news recently surfaced. At a new citizenship ceremony, one man raising his hand to swear allegiance to the very nation Khrushchev swore to bury was Khrushchev's son.

The night that Ritchie Valens, the Big Bopper, and Buddy Holly climbed into a small airplane in an Iowa snowstorm, someone advised against the flight. Holly reportedly laughed off the caution saying, "Don't you know, stars never fall out of the sky?"

Stars *do* fall. Overmuch success may not seem, at first glance, to be appropriately numbered among life's valleys. For those of us unsought by the paparazzi and unadored by the masses, whose autographs are not treasured, the burden of success seems an inviting cross to bear.

J.B. Phillips, whose translation of the New Testament sold millions of copies and whose writings and lectures inspired countless seekers, wrote of his own dreadful war with depression in *The Price of Success*. It is hard for most of us to imagine that what depresses us would not be alleviated by whatever depresses the rich and famous. We are not unlike the Mexican Chihuahua in *All Dogs Go To Heaven*. When he saw the luxurious house of a child, whom he had mistakenly believed was being kidnapped and tortured, he proclaimed, "If this is torture, chain me to the wall!"

It is hard for us to muster much compassion for a Marilyn Monroe. What could have been so bad about her life, her fame, her millions, and all her fans? What kind of valley is that? And yet it was *there*, not when she was Norma Jean, unknown and unloved, but *there* at the pinnacle of her career as Marilyn Monroe that she went into the valley of dolls and never came out.

God's Testimony in 2 Samuel 8:13-14 and Psalm 60

War had been David's life since his youth. From the moment that fateful stone had left the snug embrace of his shepherd's sling and hurtled into Goliath's forehead, he had been at war with someone. First the Philistines, then Saul, then the Philistines again, then the Jebusites, the Moabites, and even the Syrians. He seemed unbeatable. The kingdom of David extended north and east all the way to the Euphrates River. He had an occupation army in Syria and every country and king in the region poured tribute into Jerusalem.

Now he was at the peak of his career. His last opposition came from the powerful Edomites in their impregnable fortress city of Petra. To fight them in the open was bad enough. They were fierce men of the desert and, like their ancestor Esau, ferocious and petulant. To confront them also meant leading an army south among the hills of Judah, then attacking eastward in blistering heat straight toward the Dead Sea.

If they marched up the Valley of Salt, they yielded the high ground to the Edomites. But any other route was unthinkable for only there could they water the men and animals at Beer-sheba, the last well in the Negev. It was a bold gamble. If David won he would be the most famous and powerful warrior king in the Middle East. If he lost—well, *that* was unthinkable. Anyway, David was used to high-risk living and leading. Something inside him came alive in a special way when the odds mounted and the possible return was dramatic. He appointed Joab as his field marshal and headed south to Beer-sheba, then on to the Valley of Salt. His fame would either be sealed there or squandered on the rocky desert floor.

When the battle was over David knew, as did all his cheering troops, that word of the thousands, literally thousands, of dead Edomites and their Syrian mercenaries would reach Jerusalem before they did. David would be greeted with exultant triumph. From Petra nearly to Babylon, the kingdom of David was now secure. He was king: leader and warrior, the idol of men, and the desire of women. All the struggles, sacrifices, and crazy risks had paid off. War had been his life. Now he intended to return to Jerusalem and reap the rewards.

Prosperous and powerful, David contemplated where he was and how he came to be there. He was not the first prosperous and powerful king of Israel. Saul was. And in the moment of his greatest success, Saul had gone virtually insane with envy and jealousy. Violent, treacherous, and suicidal at the last, Saul had destroyed himself and his household and very nearly destroyed the nation. What had happened to Saul? Was he also, David wondered, destined to lose his soul in a season of success? The thought sent a chill down his spine. There had to be an answer.

Back in Jerusalem the question nagged him mercilessly. At last David sought release as he had so often, creatively, in song and poetry. He knew he had to commemorate the great victory in the Valley of Salt while bringing a historical and spiritual perspective to bear upon the victory. He *and* the nation needed insulation from the arrogance and insanity David had seen corrupt his predecessor and so many other successful men.

The psalm flowed out in sweet power, forming three sections. David first notes the rugged past of suffering and deprivation. Then God speaks, claiming all victory and unity as his own, from Shechem to the unity of the tribes, to the Moabites, Philistines, and Edomites. "Because of me," God says.

The psalm ends with future goals still unmet, the fall of Petra and dreams of further victories, all to be wrought only through God's help. Sung by the singers at the great victory celebration, it was greeted with popular delight, much as the victory itself had been. Whether or not the people really heard the message David meant for them to hear, he did not know. What he did know was that he was determined to receive it in his innermost being. He did not intend to end as Saul had.

The next spring, when it came time for the annual military campaign, a relatively easy one against the rebellious Ammonite city of Rabbah, David shocked everyone by staying in Jerusalem. No one objected, however. He was a king now; he did not have to fight every battle. Joab was the senior general in the army. Let him lead. David reviewed the troops from his balcony, basking in their cheers and salutes. Ah, life was good. Wasn't this what he had fought so hard for his whole life? It was time to enjoy the fruit of his success.

That night, however, David was restless and unable to sleep. He got out of bed and walked on the palace parapet in the cool spring night. There, below him in the silvery moonlight, a beautiful woman was bathing on her rooftop. He watched her, his desire rising, until she went inside.

Returning to the palace, he made inquiry about what woman lived in a certain house. At first no one was familiar with the house or the woman. Then someone spoke up. Ah, yes, *that* house. That is Uriah's house; it must be his wife. Her name, Your Majesty? Someone recollected her name was Bathsheba.

The Miscalculation of Success

I once heard a singer with the voice of an angel and the theology of a donkey. I could have listened to her sing all night, but between songs she made absolutely absurd statements of very dubious spiritual value. The miscalculation of the successful is that, since they have done well in one field, they assume they are experts in many.

Why should Ted Turner, as smart as he is about business,

think, for even a moment, that he has some meaningful theological contribution for which the world waits with baited breath? This is not to say that there are not the multiply talented, for surely there are people like Michael Jordan who had a reputable go at baseball, and Ronald Reagan, the crossover giant of all time.

It is the arrogance so common among the successful that turns men into blowhards at dinner parties, who, mocked behind their backs, never know it but go on dispensing opinions no one wants to hear. Truly admired is the neurosurgeon who listens intently to the football coach talk about his sport, and shows unfeigned interest, good-naturedly admitting his ignorance when the lady seated next to him talks about her camellias.

Key #26 to Victory in a Valley
In Success, Remember Where You Came From

I preached once for a pastor still active and full of life, who was in his late sixties. His church was booming, but his staff was sullen and demoralized. Several painful private conversations with junior staff convinced me that he was an overly demanding, unrewarding, perfectionist micromanager—a deadening combination to work for.

"Look at the way he dresses, his car, his house," one staffer observed. "Anything imperfect freaks him out. See how he's constantly checking his tie, his cuffs, his hair. Got to be perfect!"

"Do you have any insight into why?" I asked.

"Yes. He was born in Oklahoma in 1924. He was five years

old when the Depression hit, then the dust bowl. He lived his childhood in abject poverty. They had nothing! I would never have known this except for a conversation with his brother, who visited here. He said they were 'dirt-poor Okies' living in the worst poverty in America at that time. Pastor has spent the rest of his life trying to blot out that memory, trying to convince himself that poor little Okie kid with no shoes was somebody else."

All of us, to some extent or another, are the product of our past. We can be trapped by it, never able to escape the cycle of poverty, alcoholism, violence, or whatever. We can become just another part of some terrible subculture that birthed us. Or, like this pastor, we can spend our lives denying our background, wiping out every trace of it from our clothing and cars.

There is another way. Embrace the past, the good *and* the bad, and give God praise and thanksgiving for all it taught you. Some live in their past; others live trying to escape it. David wrote Psalm 60 to commemorate his great victory in the Valley of Salt, but the first three verses remember a time so hard that the people felt godforsaken and shattered by circumstances.

O God, thou hast cast us off,
thou has scattered us, thou hast been displeased;
O turn thyself to us again.
Thou hast made the earth to tremble;
thou hast broken it: heal the breaches thereof;
for it shaketh.
Thou hast shewed thy people hard things:
thou hast made us to drink the wine of astonishment.

PSALM 60:1-3

In most lives there comes a time where we feel that the only explanation for what we are going through must be the wrath of God, when the earth, shaking under our feet, threatens to break open and swallow us. The "wine of astonishment" is the beverage that leaves us with a hangover of horror. Scan the faces of the adults around you in an airport, a shopping mall, or at church. Some of those people have come from homes destroyed by divorce, violence, and drugs. Some have been raped, seen their mothers beaten, or been deserted by their fathers. Behind those faces are memories of fear, loneliness, and poverty that would make you weep to hear them.

David demonstrates that, in success, it is a good discipline to remember how it used to be. Such mental discipline will keep you humble and make you grateful. Later, in verse 6, God speaks and he says, "I will ... mete out the valley of Succoth." Mete out means to measure something and distribute it portion by portion.

What is unclear is if God means the actual Valley of Succoth, east of the Jordan along the river Jabbok, a valley that has no particular historical significance to David. There is the possibility, as well, that God is subtly reminding David and his nation, in success, to remember the feast of Succoth, an important remembrance in prosperity.

The feast of Succoth, also called Tabernacles, is a feast of rejoicing that recalls the providence of God over Israel when they wandered in the wilderness. For seven days, practicing Jews move out of their houses and into succa, which are temporary sheds, to commemorate the nation's forty years living in tents and brush arbors during the wilderness trek. Life in these succa helps to remind them of a time of total dependence on God. The uncomfortable sense of vulnerability helps shatter the mirage of well-protected, highly insured, gated-community-in-a-well-to-do-part-of-town security with which we comfort ourselves.

The feasting rejoices in God's great blessing, manna in the desert and water from a rock, that we could never get by our own getting. Gratitude for the basics—food, water, a good harvest, and survival—are crucial keys to being humble in plenty.

Succoth is the sublime combination of humility, gratitude, and celebration. It is possible to live in abundance without it corrupting us. Paul claimed that he knew how in Philippians 4:12. In America we are blessed beyond imagining. If we are to live over it, we must relearn what Paul knew, the secrets of Succoth.

Humility becomes more important the more important you become. The big shot who cannot listen to, be interested in, or learn from little shots will soon fall to arrogance. Hubris—Greek for "inordinate, arrogant, self-important pride"—is one of the major themes of Homer, particularly in *The Iliad.*

Homeric warriors guilty of such hubris think nothing can bring them down. They become implacable, unentreatable, merciless, and unteachable. A certain evangelist I admired a great deal and supported modestly had a sudden and, to me at least, totally unexpected moral collapse of Homeric proportions. I was completely blindsided. I needn't have been, however, for at least one of the telltale signs of hubris was there, if I had only opened my eyes.

After the scandal broke, I remembered a fund-raising letter that had come to me just before the news. For some reason I found it and reread his letter. In that letter he actually claimed to be God's greatest instrument in our generation. In fact, he even said that, without him, much would go undone. Now I could see it. Did he actually believe that God and the world needed him so very badly? Was he, in his own eyes, that indispensable in the kingdom?

A week in a succa can remind us that we do not need the luxury to rejoice and that God does not need us to fulfill his purposes. When you are broke and down on your luck, the Feast of Tabernacles is good. It is always good. When you are wealthy, powerful, successful, and much admired, Tabernacles is necessary!

I met a well-known comedian who was featured on a highly successful country music television show. His house was a brick mansion worthy of his newfound wealth, but in the backyard was a little wooden shack.

"Why don't you tear that down?" I asked.

"No," he said. "That's where I used to live before the show came along. I still sleep out there every once in a while to just remind myself that I could live there again if I had to. I could do it and be happy."

He was not an educated man and not a Christian that I know of. He was certainly not Jewish, but in his own Valley of Salt, where, like David, he made a name for himself, he had somehow found the homespun wisdom to remember Succoth.

Key #27 to Victory in a Valley
Always Set New Goals

A physician friend told me that he had observed so many of his friends that seemed happily married through medical school but got divorced soon after. Indeed, my wife and I, who have now been married across four decades, experienced our greatest and only serious marital troubles immediately after seminary. While we struggled to get through college, then graduate school, then the poverty of a country church, we had something to fight for. When, too young, I became the well-paid senior associate at a wealthy suburban church, we began to have troubles.

Through the years my wife and I have learned the inestimable value of a shared goal. Having reached the top of a hill, rejoice, then quickly take on a mountain. Keep moving back the horizon or run the risk of David's greatest mistake.

The last verse of Psalm 60 is a vision for future success by God's power. "Through God we shall do valiantly ..." (v. 12). He had marked the deprivations of the past, celebrated God's grace in the Valley of Succoth, and at the end of the psalm looks ahead to future achievements. If only David had listened to his own advice. The very next year "David sent Joab ... and besieged Rabbah. But David tarried still at Jerusalem" (2 Sm 11:1). It was that night that David's eye fell on Bathsheba.

Of course, we do not want to live as driven workaholics; but to rest upon our laurels, drifting purposeless in our prosperity, is far more dangerous morally. Having won a great battle in the Valley of Salt, having reached a goal or after achieving some pinnacle of personal success, quickly set a new one and move on.

Key #28 to Victory in a Valley
Give God the Glory

"For he it is that shall tread down our enemies" (Ps 60:12). A sports commentator recently complained about those professional and college athletes who, when interviewed, speak up about their gratitude to God. "I'm sick of hearing it," he said. "'I thank God for giving me the talent.' 'I want to praise God for letting me score that last touchdown.' Well, what about the other team? Why didn't God help them?"

He utterly missed the point. The issue is not that God chose one side over another, it is that in the moment of personal success, the athlete quickly turns the glory to God. He is wise to do so. Some may say that it is a superficial and insincere way to testify and that God actually gets little of the glory from the overpaid hulks, but that again misses the point. They are, at least, attempting to remember where lies the source of their strength.

Celebrate the past, set new goals, but remember, publicly and in your own heart, to give God the glory. Tell everyone that will listen how grateful you are to God for the position, privilege, and power. That will give God glory. More important, it will remind you that you are in debt for the success you enjoy.

While many live in totally selfish, and highly conspicuous, consumption, some few great athletes pour millions back into the ghetto, serve in soup kitchens, and endow college scholarships. Philanthropy is a way to give God the glory. Such giving says this came from God, he did it, not me alone, and I must use it as he directs.

This is not to say that we should do nothing and wait for the

"Jesus Blessing Lotto" to call out our name. We must train, equip the army, mount up, and ride into battle, but if we go alone it is but to fail. David and his army fought in the Valley of Salt, but he acknowledged that divine assistance is better than a sword. "Vain is the help of man" (Ps 60:11).

That is the balance between human effort and heavenly help. Proverbs puts it well: "The horse is prepared against the day of battle: but safety is of the Lord" (21:31). Go into battle without all human preparations done and you may be tempting God, but having done all that you can do, know that ultimately the outcome is in his hands.

The Conclusion of the Matter

Stretching from the Valley of Salt to the Valley of Succoth, there is one cord that connects the two. It is gratitude. Humble in need to receive help, we must then be humble in abundance to give thanks. Ingratitude is the monstrous sin of the selfish. No matter what blessing the selfish get, they feel it is only barely what they deserve, and that infrequently. Usually it is not good enough to be worthy of them. Lacking the humility to see themselves as unworthy, they lack also the grace to be grateful.

This is not a matter of gratitude to God alone, but to all those whose lives have blessed ours, including parents, teachers, spouses, and employees. A proper "thank you" is a precious commodity in an arrogant world.

I preached a very sad funeral a few years ago, that of a lady in my church, a precious saint of God who loved the Lord and was earnest about the things of God. Her husband, Henry, came to church every now and again just to get her off his back but he was a proud and stiff-necked man.

Her casket was covered with the most beautiful blanket of roses I had ever seen in my life, and there were stands of roses on both sides. It was beautiful.

I asked Henry, "Where did these roses come from?"

He said, "Well, I'll just tell you about that, Pastor. You know how Martha always loved roses. We'd be driving along and beside the road she'd see these people selling flowers and she'd say, 'Henry, why don't you buy me some flowers? Why don't you buy me some roses?' Well, I was never much into that emotional, romantic stuff. But I'm making it up to her now."

Give her the roses now! You are not going to make it up to Mom or your wife at the funeral. You are not going to make it up to your dad when he's in his casket. You are not going to make it up to God later on. There is humility in gratitude, a charming brokenness in saying, "These victories you have given me, these triumphs are from you." God loves the prosperous business man who goes into his prayer closet alone and says, "Oh, God, I thank you. I praise you for what you've done. Oh, God, you've given me wisdom. You've given me clarity of purpose. You've prospered me. But, oh, God, I know where it came from. Thank you, God. Praise you, God." God loves that man, and that man he will keep safe … even after a victory.

THE RIO GRANDE
VALLEY

The Rio Grande (Big River) is not really very big. The Mexicans call it Rio Bravo but it isn't very wild either. It's the valley that's big and wild. The Rio Grande staggers down from El Paso to Brownsville carving out a crooked and profoundly porous border with Mexico.

South through the Big Bend and on down to Del Rio, cleaving Eagle Pass, Texas and Piedras Negras, Mexico, the Rio Grande heads stubbornly south in the blazing heat. With Laredo on its left and Nuevo Laredo on its Mexican right, the river pushes down to Roma, Mission, and McAllen. Finally it splits Brownsville, Texas and Matamoros, Mexico with ragged imprecision.

Early one morning, I crossed back into the United States at Roma and headed south along the Texas side. Before I reached Mission, a green border patrol vehicle shot around me and turned on its lights. The flatbed truck in front of me careened madly onto the shoulder and screeched to a halt. Before my astonished eyes, men popped, like a truckload of jack-in-the-boxes, from all the drums in the back, and leaping down, ran into the groves on foot.

I remember sitting in my car watching those men run like rabbits among the citrus trees and thinking that borders never really work. Somebody always gets desperate to get in or to get out, then a valley running east and west becomes a highway north and south.

Ten

BACA:
THE VALLEY OF TEARS

A t a dinner party in Atlanta I introduced to each other two acquaintances of mine who had never met before. I thought my preacher friend, Carl, might be an encouragement to Peggy, whose husband had left her for another woman. Peggy was riddled with explosive anger and when she heard that Carl was a preacher, her story spilled out on him in acidic bitterness.

At last she demanded, "What does God have to say to me about *that?*"

"Lay your head on my chest," Carl said. *"That's* what God says. Pain that drives us away from God is a victory for Satan. The sweetest moments of your life may be waiting just ahead for you, not beyond but *in* this valley you're in."

I was surprised when Peggy sniffed in disgust at this and flounced away, presumably to join better listeners than Carl in another room. Later I asked her about Carl and his statements, and, though she was reluctant at first, she finally spoke her mind.

"What do I think of what Carl said? I'll tell you *exactly* what I think. I think male preachers who have never been through any real pain in their lives ought not to offer idiotic platitudes to women who are going through hell. I think he needs a little pain in his own life to make him understand what I'm going through."

"What makes you think he's never had pain?" I asked.

"Well just listen to him. The sweetest times of your life may be in *this* valley? That's a man who's never been in a valley."

"What would you say," I asked her, "if I told you that his wife was raped and beaten into a coma by a psychotic teenager? She was in a trauma ward for weeks and in physical and psychological therapy for years after that. She still limps badly, speaks with a slur, and struggles with bouts of depression when she has to stay home with a nurse—like tonight."

"Is that all true?"

"Yes, Peggy, it is," I told her. "It's *all* true. That's why I wanted you to meet him. I thought he might help you."

"No!" Peggy snapped. "He cannot help me because he is not in touch with his own hurt. Why did you think I could ever be helped by a smug crackpot living in denial?"

Why do two people pass through comparably agonizing valleys of weeping and one comes out better and the other bitter? What makes the difference? After more than thirty years of observing and ministering to people in pain, I am convinced that differences in temperament and natural disposition are insufficient to explain the disparity. So are historical details. One is *always* younger or older or richer or poorer than another but no apparent pattern evolves. The answer or answers must lie elsewhere.

Roberto Benigni's modern cinema classic, *Life Is Beautiful,* is an exuberant and poignant anthem to the triumph of the human spirit. The World War II era story is of an eccentric and jubilant Italian Jew who, along with his little son, is cast into a Nazi concentration camp. He is determined to make the horrendous experience bearable for the lad by using boundless creativity, joy, and sacrificial humor. The plan worked for the boy and the movie works for the viewer. *Life Is Beautiful* was greeted by wild critical acclaim and won two academy awards for Benigni.

Predictably though, some were outraged by what they perceived as Benigni's frivolous, even lighthearted approach to the Holocaust. Such critics certainly missed the point. Benigni was *not* saying that Nazi concentration camps were fun and games for the imprisoned. God forbid! He was creating a visual poem to the indomitable power of a joy that, even in life's most horrible moments, still says *Life Is Beautiful.* At the end of the movie, his father murdered in the camp, his country ravaged, his childhood ripped from him, the little boy finds his mother on the day the prison camp is liberated.

Leaping into her arms, the lad lifts his arms and crows in triumphant glee, "We won! We won!"

Not the valley of tears, nor all the forces of demonic darkness that assail us there, not even the pain that we must endure need defeat us. Life *is* beautiful and we *can* win. Many died in prison camps. Some died in defeat. Benigni's jolly hero died in victory.

God's Testimony in Psalm 84

How amiable are thy tabernacles, O Lord of hosts!
My soul longeth, yea, even fainteth for the courts of the
    Lord:

my heart and my flesh crieth out for the living God.

Yea, the sparrow hath found an house, and the swallow a nest for herself,

where she may lay her young, even thine altars, O Lord of hosts, my King, and my God.

Blessed are they that dwell in thy house: they will be still praising thee. Selah.

Blessed is the man whose strength is in thee; in whose heart are the ways of them.

Who passing through the valley of Baca make it a well; the rain also filleth the pools.

They go from strength to strength, every one of them in Zion appeareth before God.

O Lord God of hosts, hear my prayer: give ear, O God of Jacob. Selah.

Behold, O God our shield, and look upon the face of thine anointed.

For a day in thy courts is better than a thousand.

I had rather be a doorkeeper in the house of my God,

than to dwell in the tents of wickedness.

For the Lord God is a sun and shield: the Lord will give grace and glory:

no good thing will he withhold from them that walk uprightly.

O Lord of hosts, blessed is the man that trusteth in thee.

PSALM 84

David was a complicated man who lived a complicated life. Whose can compare? His life endured some incredible emotional intenerations. He had peaks of triumph so exhilarating that when he danced in the streets, a nation danced with him, but his valleys were canyons of unbearable grief. Is there a wound you think no one else could understand? David would have.

He went through war, exile, rejection, plague, and aching loneliness. He was betrayed by friends, falsely accused, hunted like a rabid dog, and thought to be, at times, both a traitor and a madman. His first wife married another man while he was away at war, his son stole his kingdom and raped his harem, and his brothers thought he was an egotistical liar. One of his sons died in infancy, one was a murderer, and one was an incestuous rapist. David would have understood all your griefs, fears, losses, betrayals, depressions, and despair because he endured every one of them—and more.

The complicating factor in all of his dreadful moments was that they were all mixed up together, the "deserved" and the "undeserved," until they became a Mulligan stew of a life, virtually impossible to tell what "caused" what. Many valleys David endured because of *his* sin. Some he endured because others sinned. When you are in a valley, a veritable gorge of unbearable pain, you discover that what got you there is less important than how you endure it. What "causes" those valleys of tears through which we crawl in agony, is less important than questions like, how long will it last? And, will I live through this? Will I ever be happy again?

I would love to know which particular "Valley of Baca" David had in mind when he wrote Psalm 84. Baca means *tears* or *weeping* in Hebrew. Was he remembering the bitter tears he wept for Bathsheba's dead baby? Or was it Absalom's death that still haunted him so many years later? Perhaps he was contemplating those terrible nights in hiding, alone in the cave of

Adullam, while his wife Michal was back in the city in the arms of another man.

In a way I am glad we do *not* know exactly which valley he memorialized in this Psalm. Not knowing allows us to make the Psalm fit our own valley of tears, whatever it is.

This chapter is dedicated to all those whose valley of pain is unbearable. They have told me their stories at countless altars, on a thousand airplanes, and in hundreds of letters splotched with tears. This is for the football coach from Iowa who had just discovered that his son was a homosexual, for the young widow whose husband was killed in a car crash on the way to an assignation with his mistress, and for that disoriented elderly insurance executive whose wife had *that week* been diagnosed with Alzheimer's disease. I think of the professor at a Christian college whose daughter was pregnant out of wedlock, and the backslidden Episcopal priest whose son was dying with a brain tumor, and I remember that first-semester freshman who went home for Thanksgiving break only to find her mother dead from a self-inflicted gunshot wound.

I do *not* catalogue these horrors to help anyone see that "there is always someone in worse shape than you are." I have used that counseling tactic in the past and found it scant help to the deeply anguished. I list them to embrace them and to embrace your valley of tears with them. I am convinced, absolutely, unshakably convinced of two things. First, there are valleys so horrible that in them men's souls melt like wax and women wail in the night. Second, there is comfort from God but some may find it painful even to receive it.

I once visited a man who had fallen from a construction scaffolding. Miraculously, his life had been spared, but the skeletal damage and bruising was pretty severe. While I was in his hospital room, his sister arrived. Quite understandably she rushed toward the bed.

"Don't touch him!" the man's wife cautioned her.

"Not even a hug?" the woman asked. "I just want to comfort my brother."

"Right now, Barb," whispered the shattered man in the bed. "I just can't take the comfort."

I hope this chapter will be the balm of Gilead, a healing ointment on your deepest wound. But I know that there will be those who, right at this moment, can't take the comfort. Don't work at it too hard. Let this psalm and, perhaps, this chapter bathe you with God's love for the hurting. Lie back in the gentle arms of grace and allow the waters of the Holy Ghost to wash your wounds.

Psalm 84 is precious medicine to make the hurting whole. There are three parts to the poem, steps, if you will, that can begin the healing process.

First, David testifies of his longing for God (vv. 1-3). Then he speaks to the definition and source of true happiness (vv. 4-8). Finally, David addresses the matter from a heavenly viewpoint, an obvious attempt, in his pain, to restore eternal perspective (vv. 9-12).

The True Longing of the Human Heart (Ps 84:1-3)

Any desire but the highest can be stolen from me in some dark valley. Life, liberty, love, and possessions are far more temporary than we dare to admit to ourselves. If my most passionate longings are fixed on any of these, I am primed for despair in the Valley of Baca.

In Psalm 84, David's heart is fastened where ours must be. Listen to the poet's language. His are not the take-it-or-leave-it languid verbs of twenty-first century, overfed jades who drift along a lazy, summertime river of prosperity and ease.

"My soul longeth, yea, even fainteth for the courts of the Lord: my heart and my flesh crieth out for the living God" (v. 2).

David knew about *longing*, and *fainting*, and *crying out*, knew to long for God *before* the valley, to faint for his touch *before* the weeping begins, to *cry out* before the crying starts. Like a sparrow in her nest, David testifies, I rest my soul in the altar of God, *before* I must find him in some valley of pain.

The True Happiness of the Human Heart (Ps 84:4-5)

"Blessed" is the King James version of the modern word *happy*. If my ultimate happiness rests in money or a job or even relationships, the Valley of Baca can steal it all in a heartbeat. David says true happiness is in dwelling in God, praising God, and finding God's strength—*before* you get to the valley.

Paul put it this way. We can be separated from all those things, good things, wonderful things, like homes and families, by economics so huge we cannot understand them, and viruses so small we cannot see them. But no valley can steal happiness anchored deep in heaven.

Who shall separate us from the love of Christ? shall tribulation, or distress, or persecution, or famine, or nakedness, or peril, or sword? ... Nay, in all these things we are more than conquerors through him that loved us. For I am persuaded, that neither death, nor life, nor angels, nor principalities, nor powers, nor things present, nor things to come, nor height, nor depth, nor any other creature, shall be able to separate us from the love of God, which is in Christ Jesus our Lord.

ROMANS 8:35, 37-39

David would have agreed, perhaps adding only—nor even the Valley of Baca.

The True Hope of Humanity (Ps 84:9-12)

All the trials, *and* all the blessings of this present life, cannot begin to compare to even one day in the eternal palaces of the eternal God. David frames it nicely for us when he says, "I had rather be a doorkeeper in the house of my God, than to dwell in the tents of wickedness" (v. 10).

Such an eternal perspective will keep men calm when the stock market crashes, and women sane when SIDS makes motherhood but a fleeting dream. When all this world's treasures and hurts are over, a moment in the humblest post in heaven will be more marvelous than a lifetime in the palaces of worldly pleasure.

The Miscalculation of Miserable Comforters

The book of Job is a document of pain. A man in horrendous agony is confronted by three "friends" who claim sin is the answer to his plight. One of these, Bildad the Shuhite, happily explained Job's distress to him this way:

If thou wert pure and upright; surely now he [God] would awake for thee, and make the habitation of thy righteousness prosperous.

JOB 8:6

In other words, Bildad said, if you are right with God you will always prosper. His reasoning, not uncommon even today, goes something like this. Look where the blessings are obvious and there you will find righteousness (or *faith* depending which channel of Christian TV you tune in). The reverse, such reasoning proclaims, is also true. Pain is proof of sin—or lack of faith or a negative confession. In other words, according to Bildad, Eliphaz, Zophar, and their ilk today, in God's system of justice you get what's coming to you.

I have found that such "Job's friends" reason from their own happy condition. That is, smug in their own circumstantial blessedness, they see their prosperity and health as proof of their righteousness or, at least, of their own great faith.

> Little Jack Horner sat in the corner
> Eating his Christmas pie.
> He stuck in his thumb and pulled out a plum
> And said, "What a good boy am I!"

Dear friends of mine in the ministry lost a son in a car crash. They told me that on their excruciating journey through the valley of weeping, they endured much unnecessary pain because of "Job's friends" who told them that if they had more faith, their son would never have been killed. Others told them it was due to their hidden sin or their son's.

Job said, "Miserable comforters are ye all" (Jb 16:2).

He was right! If you jam your thumb in and get a plum, remember that somebody else baked the pie *and* guided your thumb. By the same token, when the whole pie falls face down at your feet, be careful where you seek comfort.

Key #29 to Victory in a Valley
Pass Through but Don't Camp

There are equal and opposite errors with respect to the Valley of Baca. On the one hand are those particularly irritating "faith" teachers, so called, who claim that a true saint has no business in the Valley of Baca. They are not only boorish but shallow and superficial. David saw it differently.

"Blessed is the man whose strength is in thee; in whose heart are the ways of them. Who passing through the valley Baca ..." (Ps 84:5-6).

David wrote that a person who passes through the Valley of Tears is blessed! That remarkable idea flies in the face of modern, comfort-obsessed cultural religion, but it is definitely a New Testament view.

"Wherein ye greatly rejoice, though now for a season, if need be, ye are in heaviness through manifold temptations: That the trial of your faith, being much more precious than of gold that perisheth, though it be tried with fire, might be found unto praise and honour and glory at the appearing of Jesus Christ" (1 Pt 1:6-7).

No modern Christian has more graphically demonstrated a faith purified by fire than Corrie ten Boom. Can anyone imagine a valley of tears more horrifying than the Ravensbrück concentration camp? To the Nazis she lost all her possessions, her dignity, and her entire family. Was it lack of faith that put her in Ravensbrück? What an absurd thought! Or perhaps sin? Nonsense. The sins of others? To be sure. But why did *she* have to suffer? Why do any of us?

In the Valley of Baca, the question of "why" pales before the mere *fact* of the valley and its potential to purify us if we will let it. None of Corrie ten Boom's worldwide spiritual impact, her books, her sermons, her ministry, *none* of it would have been possible without Ravensbrück.

Christians, Spirit-filled Christians, holy Christians of *great* faith do pass through valleys, and valleys are not the worst thing that can befall a Christian. It is not God, but Satan, the world, and some in the church who tell us that we are getting what we deserve. If we get what we deserve, hell will not contain us all.

If we can learn to embrace the valley experience rather than question it or rebel against it, we can more quickly find the blessing. I met quite an elderly man who told of his childhood drudgery working in a Boston sweatshop. During impossibly long hours at low wages under pathetic conditions, he labored in a button factory. His favorite job, he told me, was polishing pearl buttons.

"They taught us to hold them against a grinding wheel, turning them every which way until they were perfect. I asked the supervisor that was teaching me how I would know when they were perfect. That super taught me a great lesson. When the button no longer grumbles against the wheel, no matter how you turn it, it's perfect."

Perhaps Christian perfection is when we stop grumbling against the wheel of life. The other side of this issue is equally important. While it is true that Christians must occasionally pass through valleys, they must also pass all the way through. Just as some believers grumble against the wheel, others move into the valley and turn it into a campground, even build houses there and put down roots.

The besetting sin in the Valley of Baca is self-pity. Tempted to wallow in our sorrows, we tend to camp where we should not. "Passing through the valley of Baca" is no shame, and no sign of weakness, but *pass on through*. Let time and grace do their good work. Some who go into the Valley of Baca never come out because they refuse to let go of the pain they found there. It becomes, first, a part of them, then finally, their very definition. Unable to imagine life without their hurt, they clutch it to themselves.

Some years ago a minister friend of mine met a blind lady in the Los Angeles airport. He said, "Ma'am, I am a preacher who believes in miracles. Will you let me pray for your eyes?"

"You get away from me," she snarled. "I waited on my husband hand and foot for thirty years. Well, now it's his turn."

For any one of a vast multiplicity of reasons, some enter the valley of tears against their will, but refuse to pass through. In the Valley of Baca, say it to yourself, over and over again, I *will* come out of this. I *will* come out of this! There *is* an end to this for me. I am *not* my pain. Say it when every step is agony, when you can hardly find faith to believe it yourself, but say it all the same. I am in this valley now. I will not live in denial and call it faith. But I will come out on the other side. I will not live in weak resignation and call it submission to God's will.

Key #30 to Victory in a Valley
In the Deepest Part of the Valley, Dig a Well

Dig down into who God is, into his grace and compassion. In the very worst of times, bore down into God's very best. The tendency in pain is to draw away from every touch, even God's, perhaps, *especially* God's. But in Psalm 84 David says that a source of blessedness in valleys is to "make it a well."

Notice that at the end of verse 6, David speaks to the double-sided process of grace. "The rain also filleth the pools." Rain does not fill a well. That is artesian water, underground springs that seep in to fill from the bottom up. Surface pools, tanks we call them in Texas where I grew up, are filled by rain. When we drill down into Artesian Grace, God, in his mercy, unleashes the rain upon us. The same twofold process that flooded the world in Noah's day now floods our souls with healing, inner springs from deep within and grace like rain from above.

Let me show you how it works. At the funeral of a suicide victim, I found an opportunity to speak alone with the grieving widow. I shared some basic thoughts on grace and read a passage from the Bible, and then we prayed. Pretty standard operational procedure for ministry to the bereaved. It was what *she* said that was so interesting.

"Since this happened, I have not let go of God. I have never clung to him as I have in the last two days. Night and day, night and day I just cling to Jesus. I never thought of myself as a strong person, or a very spiritual one, or even very prayerful, but I am finding inner strength and peace I never knew was there. Then God sends people like you, so many, and, I never thought about it, but all those words of love and comfort—you know what? They *do* help. They really do."

Blessed are the widows who, passing through the Valley of Baca, somehow make it a well. The widows, and the parents of the wayward, and the deserted, rejected wives, and the dying, and the lonely old man in the nursing home. Dig down. Let grace within fill the well and God will send blessed rain to fill the pools.

The Conclusion of the Matter

My son is now grown, married, and a father, but when he was a small boy, he had a friend with a terrible disease. Jason lost first one leg, then the other and, at last, his life. Travis and Jason were inseparable. They played like puppies, Jason scooting around our house on those two little stumps, laughing and romping with Travis just as boys with legs will do. Travis, large for his age, would carry Jason for hours until it was sometimes difficult to tell where one boy began and the other ended.

Little Jason was a sweet-natured child who faced his own death fearlessly and with a spirituality way beyond his years. His death was traumatic for everyone, including his family, of course, *and* Travis. We had not spoken of Jason for years until recently at a certain gathering of young adults some youthful cynic said a bit bitterly, "I've never even known a truly great Christian."

"I have," Travis said quietly. "His name was Jason."

It is not in the floodlights nor upon the stage that we prove our faith. Mountaintops of joy do not fill us with great grace because we do not need great grace way up there. It is not so much at weddings where we leave the world a lasting word about who God is, but at funerals.

THE JORDAN

Stoically leading his camels, his bedouin burnoose pulled low over his black eyes, he is an anachronism, a relic of a still-present past lingering uncomfortably amidst a modernity he cannot begin to comprehend. Our tour bus passes him headed south to Qumran, and as it does, a dozen cameras click his quaint image onto film, recorded for living room slide shows and suitable for framing.

He is in many ways typical of the sometimes violent contrasts of the Jordan River Valley, a lush agrarian ribbon laid soft against the hard barren desert. The Jordan divides Israel and the nation of Jordan, divides Jews and Palestinians, divides camel herders and BMW-driving merchants who make better use of the passersby in tourist coaches.

The river begins near the calm pools of Banias in the cool Galilee and tumbles down to baptize hordes of Christian pilgrims nowhere near where Jesus was actually baptized, south to where he actually was baptized and where now, for military reasons, no one is. It finally slides silently into the Dead Sea, degenerating into no outlet, lifeless in the blazing sun, and mute beneath the stern gaze of Masada.

How odd, how oddly human, that the Jordan, birthed in life, ends so artlessly in death.

Eleven

THE LAST VALLEY:
THE SHADOW OF DEATH

I have seen people die. I think that I have not seen so many as soldiers do, nor as many as the nurses and doctors who must attend them at the last, but I have seen enough to draw some conclusions. People mostly die as they have lived, some angry, or in great fear, or calm and sweet.

It seems strange, I know, to speak of people dying a "sweet" death or, perhaps, even an angry death, but they do. At the bedside of a prosperous, godless CPA, I watched him fight for breath as he had for money, scraping and clawing at the air, at the nurses, his wife, and, finally, at death itself. His face contorted in rage, he gave up, at last, with a final snarl and then a look of absolute horror came across his face, the very memory of which chills me even now. An angry, fearful death.

I was also in the room when an elderly saint of God named Charlie died. Having lain silent in a coma for several days, Charlie suddenly sat up in the bed and, staring across the room at a blank wall, lifted up his hands and shouted, "Oh! Beautiful!" With that he lay down and was dead when his head hit the pillow. He had lived a life of simplicity and holiness, and he died with words on his lips that were simple and holy.

How strange that we Christians, with immutable promises

that stretch beyond the grave, should so often act as though death were the worst thing that could happen to us. It is *not*. It is awesome because it is the one thing in life that no one, *no one*, not even those with "near death" accounts, has ever experienced fully and told us what to expect. We need a better theology of death. We also need a better understanding of how to be with others when *they* are dying, and of how to comfort those left behind.

We seldom see death in its "normal" state in our civilization. Our media saturate our minds with visual brutality of unimaginable proportions, but Grandma dies alone in a nursing home with no one around but the night nurse. We do not see death, as it was seen not so long ago in this country, in the upstairs bedroom. We do not gather around and say our last goodbyes. Few even attend funerals anymore. We have made death a media event to titillate the bloodthirsty, but we deny its reality. In this way, we have made the gore on the screen seem "normal" and the passing of a loved one "monstrous." How we face death, our own and the deaths of our beloved ones, may say more about us and our culture than how we live.

At the end of a life lived passionately for God, John Wesley lay dying, the room filled with grieving friends and followers. They were shocked when the great preacher roused himself and somehow found the strength to chide them. "Will you please stop this weeping? Won't someone sing a hymn?"

The people in the room obediently began to sing through their tears, rejoicing in the Lord. As Wesley drew his last breath, a trusted friend leaned close enough to hear the last whisper of a voice that had shaken his generation for God.

"The best part is, God is with us."

David saw it pretty much the same. "Thou art with me" are four of the most familiar and hopeful words in the Bible, and certainly part of the biblical passage most frequently quoted in the face of death. When I took a literature course in undergraduate school, someone asked our professor what he considered the most beautiful poem ever written. He answered Psalm 23, without hesitation.

"I never thought of you as a religious person," a voice in the back of the room called out, with an awkward giggle.

"Last year my son died. Everybody gets a little religious in the face of the death of a baby. At the funeral I did *not* want anything said about God. I did not believe in God, maybe even hated him, but my wife insisted on a priest. He read that psalm over my baby's casket and I knew it was the greatest poem ever written. It takes a subject, death, that hardly anyone has ever written about beautifully and somehow in it, God comforts even the godless—like me."

I don't remember anybody in the class giggling after that. In fact I don't remember anybody saying much of anything after that, but I do remember that "godless" young professor who met the God of comfort in the valley of the shadow of death.

God's Testimony in Psalm 23

The Lord is my shepherd; I shall not want.
He maketh me to lie down in green pastures:
he leadeth me beside the still waters.
He restoreth my soul:

he leadeth me in the paths of righteousness for his name's
sake.

Yea, though I walk through the valley of the shadow of
death,

I will fear no evil:

for thou art with me; thy rod and thy staff they comfort me.

Thou preparest a table before me in the presence of mine
enemies:

thou anointest my head with oil; my cup runneth over.

Surely goodness and mercy shall follow me all the days of my
life:

and I will dwell in the house of the Lord for ever.

PSALM 23

With Psalm 22 and Psalm 24 looming like mountains on
either side, this famous psalm is a valley of sorts *within* the
Scriptures. The two arresting psalms to the right and left of it
are Messianic, while 23 is pastoral. In Psalm 22, David describes
the horrors of the cross more graphically than even the New
Testament eyewitnesses, prophesying—or providing, some may
insist—the very words of Jesus as he hung there.

"My God, my God, why hast thou forsaken me?" (Ps 22:1).

David must have foreseen the Messiah's nightmare when he
wrote:

All they that see me laugh me to scorn:

they shoot out the lip, they shake the head, saying,

He trusted on the Lord that he would deliver him:

let him deliver him, seeing he delighted in him.

PSALM 22:7-8

Surely David was a prophet as well as a poet and that prophecy was fulfilled with amazing accuracy.

And the scripture was fulfilled ... And they that passed by railed on him, wagging their heads, and saying, Ah, thou that destroyest the temple, and buildest it in three days, save thyself, and come down from the cross. Likewise also the chief priests mocking said among themselves with the scribes, He saved others; himself he cannot save. Let Christ the King of Israel descend now from the cross, that we may see and believe.

MARK 15:28-32

David described the public humiliation of the cross.

They gaped upon me with their mouths, as a ravening and roaring lion.

PSALM 22:13

Remember, when David wrote Psalm 22, he knew nothing about crucifixion. The cross was a later Roman innovation of horror. Yet he described the horrendous strain the position puts on the skeletal structure, the body fluids collecting in the chest to drown the victim, the torturous thirst, even the nails, without ever having seen a man crucified.

I am poured out like water, and all my bones are out of joint: my heart is like wax; it is melted in the midst of my bowels ... My tongue cleaveth to my jaws ... They pierced my hands and my feet.

PSALM 22:14-16

One day David summoned the chief musician, Asaph, to the main palace and sang for him a new song. When it was finished Asaph sat silently, with tears of anguish coursing down his cheeks.

"Well?" David asked, at last. "What do you think?"

"It is beautiful, Your Majesty. Beautiful and terrible all at once. I never heard anything like it. But ..."

"But, what?" David asked.

"Who is it, Your Majesty? Who shall suffer so horribly? Surely not you! Who is it?"

"I am not sure, Asaph. The Spirit of the Lord gave me the words, so I am not sure what they mean. But I think—I know this sounds horrible—I *think* it means Messiah. I think *he* will suffer like that."

Not too many months later David again summoned Asaph to hear a new psalm. This was not uncommon, indeed, David's was a prolific talent that seemed to pour forth songs and poems of rich beauty. This day, however, when David finished, Asaph was speechless, dumbstruck by the triumphant exaltation of the new song.

"*That* is wonderful! Oh, David, what a masterpiece. I have never heard anything to so make my heart soar in the heavens! The people will rejoice in it! But ..."

"But, what?"

"Who is it, Your Majesty? Who is it that rises to the very battlements of heaven? Who is this that demands the gates of heaven be opened? That calls himself the King of Glory? Who is the King of Glory? Does this mean...?"

"Me?!" David was horrified. "Don't be absurd. Have I clean hands and a pure heart? It's Messiah! Asaph, don't you see?

Messiah will rise to this throne and the gates of heaven will open to his claim!"

"Yes, Your Majesty. Only ... only ... is this the same Messiah that was pierced, and rejected, and mocked, and tortured to death?"

"I don't fully understand it," David admitted. "But, the answer is, *yes*. It is the same Messiah. He shall suffer and he shall be crowned! What it all means ... I'm not sure. But it is the same Messiah!"

Soon after that Asaph was summoned a third time to the palace to hear yet another of King David's songs. This time when he finished Asaph was breathless.

"*That* is your masterpiece!" His voice was barely a whisper. "Your Majesty, I am no prophet but I tell you, when you and I are long gone, they will still sing that song. That is the greatest of all your works. Throughout all of human history when your name is mentioned, people will think of the one who goes with us through the valley."

"*He* also is the Messiah," David said.

"Yes!" Asaph agreed eagerly. "Yes, I see it now. The suffering servant on one side and the exalted king on the other and right in the middle, like a valley—the Good Shepherd. It is the very heart of all your psalms. It is as though the Lord is saying, I am with you in your valley to shepherd you, care for you, protect you and I can do it because I have been down through the pain and up to the heavens."

"I suppose you're right," David said, with a soft chuckle. "You can always see more in these psalms than I can. All I know is, Messiah will come. And, he will not draw back from my life—not from the needs, nor the thirst, nor even from the death. Blessed be the name of the Lord!"

"Yes," Asaph agreed. "Blessed be the name of the Lord. And from now on, his name shall be called Shepherd."

The Miscalculation of the Lonely

Solitude

Laugh, and the world laughs with you;
Weep, and you weep alone,
For the sad old earth must borrow its mirth,
But has trouble enough of its own.
Sing, and the hills will answer;
Sigh, it is lost on the air,
The echoes bound to a joyful sound,
But shrink from voicing care.

Rejoice, and men will seek you;
Grieve, and they turn and go.
They want full measure of all your pleasure,
But they do not need your woe.
Be glad, and your friends are many;
Be sad, and you lose them all,—
There are none to decline your nectared wine,
But alone you must drink life's gall.

Feast, and your halls are crowded;
Fast, and the world goes by.
Succeed and give, and it helps you live,
But no man can help you die.

There is room in the halls of pleasure
For a long and lordly train,
But one by one we must all file on
Through the narrow aisles of pain.

Ella Wheeler Wilcox

I am not altogether sure that poem is true even in the worst of human relationships but for the sake of argument, let us grant that it is. Even so, it is certainly not true of God. Lonely in our grief and pain, we may be tempted to assume that we are alone. Lonely and alone are vastly different. In the Valley of the Shadow we are *not* alone. In fact, we have to fight God off. He is so intent on being *with* us that we must put up an amazing struggle to be alone, but to do so is a terrible mistake. There is nothing lonelier than death, but in it we need not be alone. To die alone is the last and bitterest of miscalculations.

Key #31 to Victory in a Valley
Let God Into the Valley

Before we find victory in the last valley, we must, as David did, find the submitted faith to use the first person possessive. David did not say, *the* shepherd, or *a* shepherd, or even *our* shepherd. He said *my* shepherd. "The Lord is my shepherd" (Ps 23:1).

David envisioned a Savior who, between the twin escarpments of divine suffering and divine glory, is willing to walk through the valley of our very human need. He is more than willing to be *my* shepherd, to sleep where *I* sleep, to care where I slake *my* thirst, and to restore *my* soul. He is there to lead me, defend me, feed me, anoint me, and walk with me when death casts its shadow across my face. The only caveat is that *I* must let him.

There may be several reasons that some choose to walk alone just when they need him the most. The first is the most obvious. Unwilling to admit my sheeplike need for a shepherd, I may decline the comfort of his presence. I did a part of my early growing up on a sheep farm in Chesterfield, Missouri, and I have no romantic notions about sheep. They must be among the smelliest, most fearful, stupidest critters God ever made.

It is humbling to see oneself as a sheep, a needy, frightened, thirsty, fatigued, and defenseless sheep. We'd all rather be Jackie Chan than Barney Fife, but the pride that makes men stand alone also makes men do without comfort.

In the Valley of the Shadow of Death, pride can raise its ugly head just when we need God most. The waiting room of a hospital, with a loved one inside gradually slipping away, is the Valley of the Shadow of Death. When the doctor tells you that it's cancer and there's nothing you can do but go home and spend some quality time with your family. You just have a few weeks. *That* is the Valley of the Shadow of Death. Alone in your car where there used to be two, on the way home from the cemetery, *that* is the Valley of the Shadow of Death. Let God in. Plead with him to show you where and when to lie down, where to drink, and when to eat, and when to just keep on walking. Let him restore your soul, so ravaged by grief. Accept the food he puts before you while you eat and let him stand by, staff in hand, to beat back the enemies of fear and depression and loneliness.

An elderly woman in a country church lost her husband of

nearly sixty years. After the funeral, her family stayed with her for a while but, at last, the time came for them to go home. They begged her to come, too, but she was a proud woman and said she would be all right alone. She didn't need anyone! The next Sunday she told me about her first night alone in more than half a century.

"That night there come a terrible storm. The branches was a bangin' on the windows and the lights went out. I finally found a candle and got it lit, but searching around in the dark, I like to broke my leg. I was scared and lonely, but I was too proud to cry or beg the Lord. After a while, it got so bad I was shakin' all over like I was freezing cold. I got under the covers and started crying 'til I couldn't stop. Then I just said, 'Jesus, help me! Please help me.'

"Then someone came in the room and sat in the rocker. I couldn't see him real good in the dark, but he spoke to me. He said, 'Go to sleep, child. I'll sit up.' Just like that, I felt so peaceful, I just went to sleep. Now, preacher, here's my question. Do you think that was an angel?"

"No, Agnes," I said. "I don't think it was an angel. I think it was a Shepherd."

There is another reason some are reluctant to let the shepherd into the valley. Ill-informed about the Lord's attitude toward our suffering, many needlessly fear his scolding and condescension. They can almost hear him saying, if you had done what I said, behaved better, prayed more, or had more faith, you wouldn't be *in* this fix. Oh sure, *now* you want me to be your shepherd.

To paraphrase Wesley, if that is the voice of your God, then your God is my devil. The woman taken in adultery was smack in the middle of the Valley of the Shadow of Death. One word of condemnation from Jesus and she would have been stoned to death. Instead, Jesus comforted her, forgave her, and led her out of that valley and on to a new life beyond it.

On another occasion, that of Lazarus' death, we gain insight into Jesus' response to our very human grieving. Jesus actually delayed returning to Lazarus when news came of his friend's grave illness. This was to allow time for Lazarus to die and be buried. At Jesus' return, Lazarus would be raised from the dead. Jesus knew about the coming resurrection when he returned to Bethany; he was not somehow in the dark. Yet when he arrived at Bethany and found Mary and Martha grief-stricken, weeping, and hurt with him for not coming sooner, he did not scold them or draw away.

"Jesus wept."

How that brief verse invites us to call on him in the Valley of the Shadow of Death. He will not chide us over the graves of our loved ones saying, "Quit this stupid crying! Don't you understand, they will be raised when I return? Now dry it up!"

He tenderly comforts us with the hope of the resurrection, but he is not disgusted with our grief *now*. When we weep, he weeps with us. Listen to the voice of him who bears our burdens as his own. Yes, the resurrection is coming. Yes, you will see your friend, again. Yes! But today you are hurting and I hurt for you. You are weeping and I weep with you.

Are you in the Valley of the Shadow? Let him in for he is the resurrection from the dead, who, for now, weeps with the living.

Key #32 to Victory in a Valley
Walk Without Fear

The reason many believers fear death is the unknown character of the experience itself. They know they are going to heaven and in that they have faith. But the passageway is hidden to our eyes from this side and clouded in mystery.

Two great truths will lessen the fear. The first is that the One who will walk through it with us has been there before and knows the way. In the face of death, ours or a loved one's, how comforting it is to realize that Jesus will walk through this valley with us, and that he understands it. He did not just ascend like Elijah and Enoch. He did not just disappear like Melchizedek. He *died*. He went right through this same valley, right out the other side, right in to heaven, and has returned now to walk us through it.

Secondly, when we lose a loved one, we can gain hope and even joy through stripping away some of the mystery by understanding human death in its grander purpose. Babies have no sense of space and time. The mother cannot explain that she is just stepping into the next room to change clothes. The baby cannot tell the difference between the next room and another continent. Five minutes is as five years. Gone is simply gone and the baby grieves beyond comfort until she returns. But as a baby grows, it matures in concepts of space and time. When he is grown, a mother expects him to understand ideas like, wait here, I'm going into the next room to change clothes and I'll be right back.

As we mature toward heaven, we also must grow past an immature fear of death. If our departed loved ones could speak to us, they would say, wait, don't grieve so. I have just stepped into the next room to change clothes. I'll be right back.

Likewise, when it comes time for us to "step into the next room" we will not fear the passage quite so terribly. David spoke to this concept in the closing verse of the psalm.

"I will dwell in the house of the Lord for ever" (Ps 23:6).

An eternal faith reveals death as what it is, not the icy grip of the grave, but merely the doorway of a duplex. I have lived for the wink of an eye on this side and "goodness and mercy" have been mine over here. Now I will simply step through to the other side and there—*there* I will need neither God's goodness nor his mercy. For *there* I will have God himself.

The Conclusion of the Matter

I was lecturing in a small international Bible college in London when God moved on my heart one day to pray over each student in turn. I just prayed blessings. I am neither a prophet nor the son of a prophet. But when one boy knelt before me, a lightning bolt of pain shot through me and I knew this life would end in agony, knew it as I knew my own name. I began to weep, trying to hide my tears lest I disturb the young man or make him afraid.

At last, the Lord spoke to my heart in clear terms. This boy will return to his own and die for my name's sake. Pray for his strength. As I agonized about how to pray, the boy reached out and took my hands and put them on his own head.

"Pray as the Lord leads you," he said. "I already know how I will die."

Later, they told me that he was from Iran and that God had revealed to him that he must return there and embrace a martyr's death. He was so calm, so unruffled by the thought or by my tears, at least, in my presence, shedding none of his own. At the end of my prayer, before I could say "amen" he said, "And I shall dwell in the house of the Lord forever." Certainly I had heard the words countless times. Just as certainly, they had never quite touched me so.

The Valley of the Shadow of Death is not an optional experience. Walking it alone and in hopeless fear is. The Lord of Life will walk us through. Death is not as terrible as some think and "the house of the Lord forever" is far sweeter than we can imagine.

In Thailand I bought an absolutely beautiful lacquered box. The artwork was so exquisite that I could not resist it. The old man who sold it to me was a Christian, rare enough in Thailand, and a rich spirit as well.

"This little box is the end result of a thousand deaths," he explained. "First the tree must die. Then the log must die to its raw form, the planks must perish to their solitary state and suffer being sawn and shaped. Then the unpainted surface must die to remain so and endure the painful death of sanding and painting. Then, at last, it must die to me, that it may come to you. Do you understand?" he asked me.

"I don't know," I said. "But I know you are right."

"That is good enough," he smiled. "God will do the rest."

Keys to Victory in a Valley